PLAN YOUR NON-FICTION BOOK IN A WEEKEND

Write the right book: From no idea to your first draft

Dale Darley

Legal Notices

No part of this publication may be reproduced or transmitted in any material form (including photocopying or storing in any medium by electronic means) without the written permission of the author http://www.daledarley.com.

The purpose of this book is to educate, entertain and provide information on the subject matter covered. All attempts have been made to verify the information at the time of publication, and the author does not assume any responsibility for errors, omissions or other interpretations of the subject matter. The purchaser or reader of this book assumes responsibility for using this material and information. The author assumes no responsibility or liability on behalf of any purchaser or reader of this book.

ISBN: 9781502542533

Copyright © 2013-2022 / Dale Darley

All rights reserved.

If there's a book that you want to read, but it hasn't been written yet, then you must write it. Toni Morrison

Dedication

Plan your non-fiction book in a weekend is dedicated to my family, friends, and everyone who has ever been on a workshop, retreat, taken an online course, been coached, or to whom I have chatted at a random meeting, who has decided to write a book and change their lives.

Additional thanks to my book support team.

What others are saying

This is an excellent book if you wish to write a non-fiction book. It is clear and concise and takes you through the whole process, so you will be organised, inspired, and ready to write. I would certainly recommend Dale's book

Wow, what a great book to help plan out your book! Clear and easy to read is what I love about this book. Packed with so many tools and worksheets. No excuses for not writing your book with this little helper by your side.

Such an informative and well set out book which has helped me structure my writing/time/chapters and see where I was going off at tangents. Well worth the purchase

Table of Contents

Plan Your Non-Fiction Book In A Weekend	- 1 -
How To Use This Book	- 9 -
Why Do You Want To Write A Book?	- 27 -
Resources And Costs	- 41 -
Timings	- 57 -
How Will You Publish?	- 71 -
Getting Ideas	- 77 -
What Is Your Story?	- 89 -
Getting Clear – Values To Vision	- 103 -
Understanding Your Competitors	- 139 -
Who Do You Want To Inspire?	- 149 -
The Book Blurb And Titles	- 161 -
Your Book And Business Strategy	- 171 -
Let's Get Brainstorming	- 179 -
The Heart Spot	- 193 -
Creating Outlines And Frameworks	- 197 -

The Knowledge Audit	- 215 -
Interior Design	- 223 -
Before You Start Writing	- 233 -
Write Your First Draft	- 245 -
Turn Your Book Into A Business	- 253 -
About The Author	- 267 -
Resources	- 269 -

Plan Your Non-Fiction Book In A Weekend

In this book, I will teach you **how to plan your non-fiction book**. You will go from no idea to THE idea and have your first draft written. This will pull all the planning pieces together and give you the first draft to edit. From there, you can publish and use your book to build your brand and create other products and services.

I would like to inspire you to trust that you have something valuable to share and trust the process. If you have ever wondered how to get started on **becoming a published author** and writing a non-fiction book, then this book is for you. If you have been writing your book for a while and it is now a mess, this book is also for you. It will help you get back to basics, untangle what you have already written and put you on the right track.

The BEST way to write a book is to plan it out first. Many people don't write books because of 'stuff' in their heads; if they took the time to plan it, most of the stuff would be dealt with. This book provides you with the tools and a process to do that. It all becomes much easier when it is planned and in chunks.

Plan your non-fiction book in a weekend takes you on a reflective journey which aims to help you grow as a writer. You will not just be going through the mechanics of planning a book. You will also be provided with practical suggestions to help you generate ideas, find the right idea, create your unique planning process or methodology, and write your first draft.

It seems rather simplistic to say that you need a book on planning to help you to write. Surely, to write, all you need is a pen and paper.

If I am going on a walk with my dogs, I know where I am going, which route I am taking, and how long I have for the walk. I also plan a whole range of other things: the right footwear, outer clothes, pooh bags, tissues, and doggy biscuits. For a short walk, I can stuff my pockets with the essential items. For a long walk, I pack my rucksack with the more important items.

If, on the other hand, I am going somewhere to deliver a workshop, my planning is much more involved. For this trip to work for me, I need to write a to-do list and start making considerations for the journey long before heading out of the door. For a trip in the car, it is easy to pack a suitcase full of things just in case, whereas if I am going on the train, much more thought is needed to make my trip as easy as possible.

Likewise, with your writing, if it's a note to your partner to say "please put the rubbish out", it is very simple. If, on the other hand, you are writing a report on "the sustainable household", you may need to think about:-

- How you are going to find evidence to back up your proposal
- How to find the time for research or for interviewing a few experts
- How you will fit this report in with other activities
- Who might read it
- What action do you want them to take as a result of reading it?
- When the deadline is
- Writing and publishing a book is no different. If you plan it well, the rest (writing and publishing) becomes easier.

Quite simply, you plan to make it _easy_ to reach your destination of becoming a published author. The good news is that you can produce a great plan in just a weekend. You then undertake any of the planning advice I offer over *a series of weekends* until it's time for that all-important first draft, which you can also tackle during the week or on the weekends

You have probably read all kinds of books which promise that you can write a book in 2, 10, 20 or 30 days, and perhaps you can. What I know is that if you plan it, you can make it easier and quicker to complete.

All I ask is that you consider the advice I offer here and use it to write a book which will build your credibility, honour you and your brand and equip you with an asset you will be proud to put your name on.

There will be times of frustration, overwhelm and confusion. That is good; it means you have tickled your grey matter. Just allow your brain some space to reconnect the pieces. On days like these, put on your wellies, go out, and jump in some puddles.

This book does not promise to write your book for you. It provides a **guide to planning your book journey so that writing your book becomes easier for you** and you arrive at your destination stress-free and ready to rock.

I don't come from the school of one-size-fits-all; there is no set formula for every writer; there is *your* formula. Work through the book in your own way, try things on for size, take a few steps, see what it feels like to head in that direction, reflect on what I ask you to do, reflect on what you actually *do* and then take a few more steps.

If you are the kind of planner who likes to jump in feet first, you will know who you are. You jump off the bus because you see something out of the window that you would like to explore. As the bus pulls away, you realise you have left your shopping on the seat. Remember that at some point, you will need to hop on another bus to get home.

Planning your journey is rarely a straight line, so if what you originally thought you were going to write about changes, great, keep at it until you hit your sweet spot. You will be pleased that you took this time out to plan.

To get the best value, skim the book before you start and then go back through it with your action log roadmap and choose your best weekend for planning.

Writing is a wonderfully non-conscious act that allows you to download your insights onto paper or disk. Planning is a combination of conscious and non-conscious thinking and creativity. Once the planning is out of the way, and you have the book in front of you with each chapter outlined, you will be ready to write.

When you get to the writing stage, keep your outline in front of you with what questions you will be answering and stay focused. If you just cannot start, then you probably have not done all the *'getting clear on which book'* work. When that happens, go back to the drawing board and find something you do want to write about. Alternatively, it may be that you just need to start with a chapter other than chapter one.

Writing a book is good for your business and adds an extra dimension to your credibility as an expert, but more than that, it is good for you. You may, of course, not be writing a book for your business; this non-fiction book may be about your life and experiences – a memoir. Either way, publishing your book is an amazing way to connect to the heart of who you are and reach out to others.

We each have a purpose, a reason for being, something that we are here to deliver. As our lives unfold, our knowledge and experiences grow and deepen. When we are living on purpose, then opportunities for our purpose open. Life on purpose is about being connected to our authentic self, the one who is most creative, intuitive, passionate, links to the big picture, and is values-based. It is what we love doing without thinking. I believe that the true reason we write is that we are teachers. Just how you got to today probably came with some tough decisions and some equally valuable lessons. If you could identify your most critical challenges and how you overcame them, what lessons could you pass on to others so they could learn from you?

Your book will come from understanding what you have learnt, or in some cases endured, and knowing what drives you. When the books we write align with who we are, what we share becomes more meaningful, inspiring others to transform and expand. Knowing your book's purpose is the baseline for your plan, the heart of the book, and the bit you need to keep coming back to, ensuring that your book is on target and aligned with its original intention.

There is a huge change happening as more people take control of their content and decide to share their expertise, skills, knowledge, experiences and passion. Each year the number of self-published books increases. You are part of the revolution.

Planning creates space. Space provides freedom. Freedom allows creation.

To help you create your book, I am going to answer these essential planning questions:-

- What kind of planner am I, and how can I make the best use of my planning style and resources?

- Why you want to write a book
- What is the process and cost of writing and publishing a book?
- How long will it take me?
- How will I publish it?
- How do I get ideas for my book?
- What is my story, and how can I use it?
- How can I get clear on my values, passion, purpose and vision before I write?
- Who are my competitors, and why is this important?
- Who am I writing for?
- Sorting out a book title and the blurb
- How do I align my book and business strategy?
- How do I choose the ONE big idea for my book?
- What is an outline, and how do I create one?
- How can I use existing content
- How can I structure my chapters?
- How do I get to the first draft?
- How can I build a business around my book?

Take heed of the advice. You will have your entire book planned, own your writing schedule, personal 'getting your book done' methodology, a book action plan and be on your way to your first draft. You will be writing, planning, and reflecting, using new tools to create ways of working that make writing your book easy and stress-free for you.

How To Use This Book

This book is a guide for you to use in the best way that suits you. We all work in different ways, and what seems like a workable approach for me may not work for you. It is full of advice for you to try; you will get the best out of *Plan your non-fiction book in a weekend* by following some or all the advice and creating ways of working that are unique to you. My role is as a guide, giving you resources so you can be inspired to act.

Completing Your Book Plan In A Weekend

Skim read to get a flavour of what it is about. Reflect on each chapter and think about what works for you. The book is about firstly creating a book plan that works for you in a weekend. Then inviting you to move your schedule around and make time to write your book over several weekends.

The first step is to skim-read this book with a journal and create a plan for yourself

If you want a ready-made plan, sign up here dale-darley.ck.page/pynfb-resources

To get clarity, re-read the plan several times before your planning weekend.

Put aside some dedicated time, read through the plan and get to grips with what needs to be done

Go through each of the steps and familiarise yourself with the activities

Chunk the activities into bite-sized pieces, recognise what you can do and go for it. Leave the rest for another day

Get rid of any distractions and let others know that you are otherwise engaged

At the end of the weekend, take some time to reflect

Once you have reflected, come back and update your plan. **This is now your ACTION plan**.

The first part of the book is to get you to consider things that will help you to create a plan.

Then we move on to ideas, your story, vision, who you want to inspire, book titles and blurb, and strategy. These chapters will help you with your plan because when you consider them, you will have to think about how they will go into your plan.

The book takes you one step further and shares with you a brainstorming chapter to get your book ideas and outline out, tips on how to write your book and how to use your book to create a business.

It would also help if you felt motivated and ready for action

Plan, Plan, Plan

The key to getting your book started (and finished) starts with a good plan. By creating a comprehensive and workable plan, the rest, as they say, will follow.

By planning, it makes writing your book easier

With a plan, you are more likely to publish your book

Planning will help you stay on track

Journal

Journaling is one of the most powerful and effective ways to clarify your thoughts. I encourage you to buy a journal and to write daily. Find the right time of day to read this book, and then use your journal to record whatever comes up for you.

Create your perfect reading, journaling, and reflecting environment. A few days after you have journaled, read what you have written and let the thoughts come; these are your "aha" moments. Reflect and decide what to do. Take your time; this is your journey. Start using your journal before your planning weekend, during and after. It is, as I say, a powerful habit that can only serve to help you. That's it, simplicity itself.

Check Your Progress

Always celebrate how far you have come, not how far you have to go. Use the end of each chapter to check how far you have come on this journey.

The book is presented to you as a linear process and designed for you to follow in a systematic fashion. However, if you don't work like that, dip into the parts you need as and when possible.

Please take some time to understand yourself and how you like to work; trying to shoe-horn you into my way of thinking may not work for you, but you need to **notice how you get things done** and work by **flexing your style**. Work in a way that suits you and ensures you reach your objectives in the realistic timeframe you set.

I have clients who can easily plan from start to finish. Others start with great enthusiasm, plan the first few chapters, get bored, do a bit of scribbling, reflect, plan a few more, get bored, and then reflect again. Where people cannot work in a linear fashion, we construct a way of working that helps them recognise their patterns and put into place systems, methods, ideas, and processes that will work.

I cannot stress enough that although this book is linear and a process, it is written for you to use in your own way. If you follow it, you will get a plan for your book completed in one weekend.

About You As The Planner, Writer And Editor

Have you ever stopped to consider **how you like to learn**, what steps you take to get things done, and why you work the way you do? To be more productive and effective, we need to understand ourselves and the habits or patterns we have formed.

When working with clients, my job is to get the best out of them. It's important that I understand their learning and thinking styles so that I can plan individual strategies to ensure that they get their books planned, written and published.

> **When you begin to write your book, it is vital that you understand your preferences, as this will help you get started and finish and get published.**

Aspects of planning, writing and editing your book will be easier for some than others because each of us has preferences for how we think, learn and do.

Our ways of thinking feel a 'natural' part of us. You may be unaware of these non-conscious patterns until you learn to recognise them. You can learn to recognise them through your language and behaviour. **This is often why book projects fail – people simply do not know why they may feel overwhelmed or lose the motivation to write. It's all down to your preferences.**

Preferring a pattern of behaviour can be very beneficial when that pattern is useful in a particular context. On the other hand, you might find it difficult to adapt your behaviour, even when that way of doing something could be more beneficial. Consider how being more flexible with your thinking and behaviour may lead to more productive outcomes.

This section is not designed as a psychological tool but more of a reflection of how I have observed myself and my client's work and a review of different thinking and learning style literature. You may recognise bits out of each area, or you may strongly identify with one. This is a guide – by understanding yourself, the chances are that you will be better equipped to get what's in your head out, onto paper and through to final publication.

Whatever you do, or however you like to work, do one thing: create a plan or outline of your book before you start to write. You will be pleased that you did.

Ask Yourself A Few Questions:

When you go on a journey, do you:

- Ask a friend for directions?

- Plan the route?
- Use a printed map and/or your sat nav?
- Just head in the general direction; you know that you will get there

When you have something new, do you:

- Read the instructions first?
- Head to YouTube to watch how someone else does it?
- Ask for help?
- Just have a go (you are the ones with the leftover screws)?

When you learn something new, do you:

- Watch and learn before you do?
- Talk it through with someone first?
- Read it through, think about it for a while, and then have a go?
- Just jump in and try?

You see, we are all different, and there are reasons why some bits are easier than others. The point is to learn why you do what you do, try to flex your style or adapt how you do things, and ask for help. Everyone has to learn how to flex their planning style to get their book written and get to know and love their writing style to engage and communicate with people who are not like them.

A, B, C and D people

We are all different. Which are you?

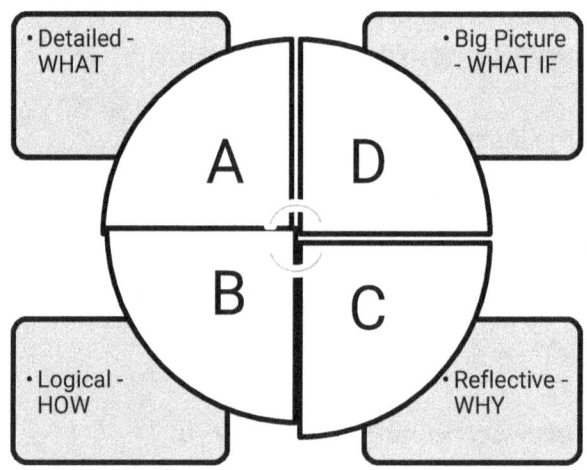

A – 'WHAT' people

You – what do I need to learn?

Your motivation comes from inside you

You are logical, factual and results-driven

You need to research and analyse the facts

You are not easily distracted, and you find it easy to focus on an activity for a set period

You are a good time manager

Environment

You like to work alone and in the quiet, without clutter or distractions

Planning

You like to gather all the information together before starting

You like clear guidelines and facts so that you can determine what tasks need to be done and by when

You can set achievable goals and are realistic about what needs to happen to get them done

You test out how many words you can write / edit in an hour or day and plan accordingly

You think through the pros and cons of how your writing project methods will work

Writing style

You are good at summarising, are concise and to the point

You apply your logic, critically evaluate what you are writing and use facts to support your theories

You tend to write more about 'what', than 'why', 'how' or 'what if'

To get the best out of your writing project, gather everything you need before you start, create a plan of how you will get it done, gather your research, time yourself to find out how long it will take and then set aside blocks of time to write. Write a set amount each day, moving through your project in a linear fashion.

Create a master plan and write it up as if it were a training course, and test the flow until it makes sense and is logical to you. Once you have it all together, talk it through with someone else to test your ideas and flow and make your content more concrete. Undertake research so that you have your facts together before you start to write.

B – 'HOW' people

You – how will I learn this?

You are very practical and hands-on

You want details before acting or making decisions

You are usually on time with your projects and plans

Environment

You are neat, orderly and prefer quiet

Planning

You are disciplined, detailed, and methodical, and you like to know that there are proven methods

You are highly organised, structured and like a step-by-step approach, with checklists and to-do lists

You like to try things to understand how you can get your plans achieved

You like planning and having a timetable to work to

Writing style

You are very detailed, factual and clear. You would be good at writing how-to and manuals

You tend to write more about "how", than "why", "what" or "what if"

To get the best out of your writing project, gather everything you need before you start and read the methodology to get a clear idea of what you must do. Create a plan of how you will get it done, make checklists for each stage and write out a flowchart (list or visual) so that you can keep checking that you are on track.

Both A and B

Organise your working environment and let others know that you have a project to complete; otherwise, distractions will drive you mad

Create your book outline with checklists for what must be covered, and keep these to hand

You may find that you will be hard on yourself if your plans do not work out the way in which you planned them. Remember to allow for distractions

Try not to get bogged down in detail. Otherwise, you will never finish planning and writing. When you edit, forget perfection; use an editor to polish your work and publish. You can refine it later following a period of sales and reflection. Your job is to make plans so that writing and getting to publication is easier for you

Working with a writing buddy or coach will ensure that you do not get bogged down in detail and will help you to move through your project

C – 'WHY' people

You – why do I need to learn this?

You are outgoing, sociable, emotional and feeling. You love to work with others

Your values are important, and you like to do things based on how you feel

You tend to need to check with others before doing things

You are great at sharing ideas

Environment

You want to be with other people and don't mind noise or music when you are working

Planning

You start enthusiastically and work intuitively but may not finish, as you are easily distracted

You have loads of ideas but have trouble picking 'the' one

Writing style

You are very creative, expressive and use emotional language

You put in case studies and stories to connect emotionally to your reader

You use creative and emotional language

You tend to write more about 'who' than 'how', 'why', 'what' or 'what if.'

To get the best out of your writing project, brainstorm ideas and work with someone to choose 'the' writing project for right now. Use a writing buddy or coach to keep you on track with this one.

Create a master plan and walk over the steps to get a feel for the flow and content. Write it up as if it were a training course. Once you have it all together, talk it through with someone else to test your ideas, flow and make your content more concrete.

Start where it feels right. You will find it hard to work in a linear fashion and will want to mix up what you do so that it always feels fresh and new

Ideas will come to you as you work, and you tend to go off track, which is why a coach is important to you

You will get frustrated with your inability to stick to one project and will want to talk about why this book will never see the light of day. Once you have reassurance, you will get back to working again

D – 'WHAT IF' people

You – mmm what if?

You are very curious about all sorts of things, which can lead to being easily bored and distracted. Your insights send you off in different directions

You want the big picture, are very visual and hate details

You keep questioning what you are working on all the time

You need constant change and variety and want to find different ways to do things

You want to do it your way

You visualise the facts; that is, you need to see things before you can make sense of them

Environment

You like an informal, casual and fun place to work, surrounded by lovely things

Planning

You hate to be held to a timetable and tend to be unstructured

Mind mapping works for you, as you need to see pictures of how it will work

You must have options for different ways to tackle your project

Writing style

You are creative and use colour, diagrams and visuals to get your point across

You often forget the details and find it hard to get past the big picture, conceptual, visionary stuff

You tend to write more about 'what if', than 'how', 'why', or 'what.'

To get the best out of your writing project, brainstorm ideas and set up visual systems so that you can see what needs to be done. Use mind maps or post-it notes so that you can move things around until they look right to you.

Create a master plan and walk over the steps so that you can see how it flows and how the content would fit together. Write it up as a mind map and put it where you can see it.

You will find it hard to work in a linear fashion. Set your outcome for finishing so that you have a deadline in your mind's eye; chop up your writing project and find options that work for you.

As you work, check off your mind map or visual with coloured pens. Then, create your outline, already set up and formatted, so you can see your writing coming together as you go along.

As you are easily distracted, when you come to writing a section, draw the diagram of what you want to explain first so that you can keep referring to the point you want to make. Remember to include details for those people who may find a picture confusing.

You will get frustrated with your inability to stick to the one way of working and will want to play around with your map for getting your book done until you see a new way of getting that bit completed.

Both C and D

Organise your working environment so that it feeds your senses. Try writing in different places when the mood takes you. Turn off your phone and the Internet and get into the habit of working for an hour and then taking a break

Create your book outline using visuals and checklists; keep them handy so that you can refer to them so that you will stay on track

Remember, other people need more detail; they might not care for case studies or pretty pictures

Get someone to help you with planning and staying on track; use an editor to be brutal with your tendency to overwrite and a coach to support and keep you on track

Everyone

Get your working environment right for you

Understand your preferred way of working and behaviours

Understand your capabilities (what skills, abilities and competencies you need to do the task) and outsource what you cannot or will not do

Get your head around what you believe to be the right way and find the best way for you. Ask, what is important to you?

Understanding yourself will help you to find a way that works for you

Keep coming back to the purpose of your book as your guide for completing this project

Don't be too hard on yourself

Actions:

Decide what kind of planner you are

Work to your capability; flex your style where you can

Set up your workspace (your environment) and decide the best times in the day that works for you – and go for it!

Read the book and download the worksheets before your planning weekend

Be brutal with your time, chuck and prioritise your activities

Have fun

Why Do You Want To Write A Book?

In this chapter, we explore your motivations to write and publish a non-fiction book. It may seem a bit obvious that you want to write a book; otherwise, why are you reading a book about planning a book? What I mean is that it is important to get clear about *why* you want to write, *what* you want to write about, *how* you will make it all happen and *what if* you and *what if* you didn't?

Why Do You Want To Write A Book?

When you have clarity, you can define where you are heading with your writing. In finding out about ourselves, we start to gain clarity of purpose. What you are passionate about and the purpose of your writing goes hand in hand. Your readers will have expectations. Your role as a writer is to make sure those expectations are met while at the same time fulfilling the purpose of your writing. Getting clear on your "why" will help you gain this clarity.

Today a business book adds an extra dimension to your credibility as an expert. It allows you to demonstrate your expertise, skills, knowledge, experiences and passion. A business book can support your workshops, help you develop other products and services, and be a highly effective marketing tool.

The business benefits include a raised profile, more speaking engagements, opportunities to collaborate with others and options for you to productise your book into online programs. Imagine seeing your voice, thoughts, ideas, concepts and words in print.

Reasons To Write A Book

Competence

Whether you know it or not, you are an expert. The trouble is, you probably take all your knowledge, skills and experience for granted and assume that everyone else can do what you do too. They can't.

Credibility

A book gives you a level of credibility that nothing else can. It is proof that you are an authority on your subject. It will help you establish yourself as an expert and earn you respect.

Competitive advantage

We all have competitors; I bet only a few have written and published books. Your book will give you an 'unfair advantage.' Plus, this ONE THING can turn into many things and provide you with a treasure chest of resources.

Change agent

Your words inspire others and demonstrate to them that they can do or achieve whatever you are writing about.

Connect

Your book connects you to others who need to hear your words and others you can work with.

Convert – leads to customers

A book is a brilliant marketing tool. It is more than your business card; it makes an introduction like no other. It works for you whilst you sleep and prepares your market for you.

Commercialisation

Your book is only one way to say what you do. Following publication, you can launch in many different ways to demonstrate this. That could be workshops, online courses, videos, mastermind groups, webinars, live streams, blogs, or programs; the ideas are endless.

Confidence

Going through the fear and lack of self-belief process and coming out the other side as a published author is amazing for your inner confidence.

Cathartic

Writing in any form is cathartic. Even when writing a book for your business, you will tap into parts of yourself that you may not have considered.

What Kind Of Book Fits Your Why?

Write a book, someone says. You have so much knowledge and skills, and what about all your amazing experiences – they say. You're delighted that someone might think you worthy of such a role inwardly beam. But in reality, it can seem like a mammoth task unless there is a more than a good reason to write. Planning and writing a book takes time and resources, so it needs to be justified in some way. You need to know your why.

Exploring why is a good place to start, but something often

overlooked is what kind of book one should contemplate writing. It's worth noting that you can write many kinds of books. I believe some books want to be written for different stages of your life. Here are a few examples to get your creative juices flowing.

The How-To Manual

The how-to manual book is the kind of book that you would write if, let's say, you taught or coached a technical subject. In the early days of my IT training career, I wrote many a how-to book. We called them training manuals. They are extremely valuable. Naturally, many people head over to YouTube to find out how to do something, which gives you an opportunity to extend the reach of your book.

Think about some of the books you own in this genre. I have one on how to use my camera and some on painting and drawing. In these, there are no stories or case studies. They simply show you have to do a particular task.

Look at some that you might own and ask, is this something I would like to do and is this something that would prove useful to my clients? For example, if you are a trainer, giving a client a how-to book (manual) as part of a training course looks far more professional than a manual in a folder. In addition, because of print on demand either from a printer or your POD publisher, you can easily keep these up to date. Plus, you have opportunities to sell workbooks and planners.

Self-Help Non-Fiction Book

In this category, it can be any kind of self-help book, be that one on personal branding, how to write a book, healing trauma, training dogs, renovating furniture and a multitude of other subjects. I've clubbed them together, whereas, on your online publisher, they would be classified by genre, e.g. business or mind, body, spirit. The essence is the same they support the reader on a journey. They differ from a manual which is more about giving instructions around a specific product.

This is where I believe you would want to ensure that your book, brand and business are aligned and that you pay attention to what this book will bring you. It must be the right book for right now. If it takes the average writer a year to 'knock out' a book while running a business and juggling life, then this book needs to be focused on what you want to be known for.

For example, with three other coaching colleagues, we wrote a book on Executive Leadership. At the time, it was relevant for all of us. My life changed, and although I am extremely proud of it, it's not currently as relevant for me as the other authors. By comparison, this book is still as relevant to me as the day I first published it.

What do you love doing, what are you good at, what does the world need and what can you be paid for? What do you want to be known for which is sustainable in, let's say, two years?

Memoir

A Memoir is a slice of your life. Memoirs are written for many reasons, most notably to leave a legacy. Everyone has a story or two to tell, but whether they want to tell it is another story. It requires a theme and a purpose. If you are writing about another family member or another person, that is a biography.

Again, memoirs fall into many categories, trauma, finding yourself, adventure or maybe a dedication to a cause. When you find yourself in a life-changing position, writing your story for you and your intended reader is empowering and healing.

This kind of book tends to be written by people who use it to support their speaking careers or raise awareness of an important issue, but equally to contribute to their business in some other way.

Self-Help Memoir

I've separated this from a normal memoir, as I see this as a combination of a self-help book and memoir that you would use for your business. Your book would chart a period of your life, tell a story, and offer research, practical experience and advice.

If you have experienced something life-changing and now want to coach and consult in this area, a book written like this is a) very rewarding to write and b) adds credibility to your brand and c) is something you can build products and services around. And it could be your business pivot book.

Healing Memoir

These books are what I call healing books, and their sole purpose is to help you and others to heal. They typically start as a journaling and writing to heal part of the process.

This book may never see the light of day, although I hope you do publish it. You have been through a trauma of some kind, healed from an illness or deep emotional scars and want to move on. While there are many therapies that you could choose, writing is known to support healing. You could argue that journaling would serve the same purpose, and it might. However, with a healing memoir, you are following the flow of planning and writing a 'normal' non-fiction book or memoir, but instead of writing to publish, initially, you are writing to heal.

What is fascinating is that these stories will want to be shared at some point, and you will know why and when. So if you are reading this and the thought of publishing does not sit with you, I invite you to write your story anyway and ask for guidance on when to publish.

When the healing phase is over, you would reflect and then consider how to publish this and how you would use it like the other self-help books to help others to heal.

Often what works best is to work with a coach who would guide you through the process. Each week, you would meet to discuss the chapter and pour yourself into your book. Talking and writing with purpose enables you to explore your story, gain perspective, and heal.

I have worked with many people in this way. The book might not get published immediately, but it is one of the most rewarding writing to heal experiences I know of. My favourite way of publishing this is to make it a self-help healing memoir.

Biography

A biography is a story about someone else or something else. Perhaps you are a fan of a particular band, a family member was held in a prisoner of war camp, someone made a heroic journey, a person you want to write about suffered adversity, cured an illness, or went on a remarkable adventure.

I see these books about preserving the history surrounding the event and possibly not something that would support your business but would nonetheless be extremely rewarding.

Which will you choose?

Whichever you choose, remember it will only get written if it speaks to your heart. Where writing is concerned, nothing gets done if it feels like you have been airlifted into purgatory.

I also believe that you must ensure that your book, brand and business are aligned and pay attention to what this book will bring you. It must be the right book for right now.

Your 'Why' And 'So What' Questions

To start the process, ask yourself why you want to write a book?

The Five 'Why's' Or The Five 'So What's'?

A great way to get deep to the heart of your book is to ask the five 'why's' or the five 'so what's'. The trick here is to ask 'why' or 'so what' and then ask it again until you have clarity. Ask your five 'why's' or 'so what's'.

Reasons Not To Write

If you are wondering if there are any reasons not to write a book, there are.

You think writing a book will make you rich and famous

You think you will earn a lot of money so that you can leave your day job. You may be able to. However, it will be from the business you build around your book and message

Everybody else is writing a book, so you should

You want to impress others

If these are some of the reasons you have chosen to write a book, you might as well stop now because they are not real motivators. If you are not motivated and have no passion for the subject, your book will never be written. Don't write a book to prove anything to others. Write it because you want to maximise the learning experience and because it will add value to *you and others*.

Why your book?

Do you feel your story or business concept has been explored and told a thousand times? Think of all the films you have been to see. So many seem to be similar, yet there is a central idea that is different, that takes us by surprise and has us gripped, right through to those final moments when THE END comes, and we are left sitting staring at a blank screen, wanting more. Unlike a film, we cannot add special effects or thrilling sounds, but we can add the things that make it different, according to you. When you share something that gives you purpose, it can only serve to inspire others who read it.

Ask yourself what you want to **feel** when you read your book. What do you want others to feel? Excitement, passion, the familiarity of sipping tea with an old friend, in tune with the conflict and energised into action? What do you want them to know or do?

How on earth, you may ask, can you create a unique book when so many people have been ill, divorced, climbed a mountain, been abused, sick and healed, travelled the world, built businesses and are experts in your domain……?

What makes it different is your take on it, your inner vision and wisdom, how you did what you did, and how you convey your inspirational message and purpose to the reader.

Exercise: Your book idea

Take a sheet of A4 paper, fold it in half, and create 'your book.' Write up everything *except for the blurb* before you go to bed. Pop it (your book) under your pillow and *write up the blurb in the morning*. When it is completed, reflect in your journal.

Front

Your book title – write the first thing that comes into your head.

The inside is split into three parts.

Inside 1

WHAT: what is your book about? What will your client/client get from reading it – their outcome?

Inside 2

WHO is your reader? Draw a picture and brainstorm some of their needs and problems.

Inside 3

WHY: why are you writing it? Why will your client want to read it?

Back

THE BLURB: The stuff is on the back; it is your sales copy. Tell us about your book. Make sure it engages the emotions so that you connect with your ideal client.

This activity pulls together your thinking about your story and what you will share with the world in one place and provides more tickling of the grey matter and clarity.

Actions and Checklist

Ask:-

What is your 'why'?

What would be your reason be <u>NOT</u> to write your book?

Do the 'your book idea' exercise

Resources And Costs

This chapter is where you start to put some thought into the book roadmap. Here you will look at the process of writing a book, the resources you need and the likely cost.

The Process Of Manufacturing A Book

The product development pipeline is the future lifeblood of any business. Bringing the best products to market can lead to amazing rewards. So, for a moment, stop thinking about your book as a book. Instead, think of it as a product you will manufacture for others to consume, which will add value to their lives and business. In my experience, the most successful people are those who:

- Create and deliver products or services which meet the unmet needs of their target market
- Deliver meaningful experiences
- Understand that the market doesn't just want one thing; it needs a range of things – books, online courses, coaching, etc.
- Are doing it differently, in a way that can't easily be replicated
- Are constantly innovating, not necessarily making significant changes, but working on feedback to improve the experience and add more value
- Keep their eye on their current and potential competitors and seek collaboration opportunities
- Price it right – they think cost, price and value
- Make their products accessible, easy to buy and consume
- Consider what else the book can become and how it will

support their business

Consider These Potential Stages

The R&D and manufacturing process

- **Concept** – you have an idea(s) for a book
- **Idea screening** – as different ideas come, you brainstorm and spend a lot of time reflecting. In addition, you are undertaking some additional research, looking at competitors and your micro and macro environment
- **Concept development and testing** - you chat it over with your family, friends and colleagues, maybe even mapping your book idea out. You may also, at this stage, chat to a coach
- **Product development** – now you are working on getting your prototype ready – outlining and writing the first draft
- **Testing** – you give it to your proofreader, copy editor, beta readers or maybe a friend, who pulls it apart and gives you feedback; this takes you back into development. You may even test the market by writing a few blogs to see if anyone has any appetite for your ideas and concepts
- **Final production** – following feedback, the book goes through final edit, formatting, proofing, and the cover is created. It is now loaded up onto your online publisher (print on demand and digital) platform, ready to sell
- **Production costs and resources** – I have read and

guestimated that it takes approximately 700 hours to produce a non-fiction book. For someone who does it all themselves, a simple calculation will tell you how much it would cost if you paid someone (yourself) by the hour. Read on to find out more about the costs involved.

However, think of the VALUE that the book brings, the other products and services you can develop, and the personal development you get. Add credibility and opportunities, and wow!!

Marketing

- **Pricing** - consider what price your book will sell for. What is your break-even figure, and what other ways can you create sales from it so you can recoup your costs? Remember that this book can be used as a lead generation tool, and therefore the price you set becomes somewhat irrelevant
- **Commercialisation** – once it has been published, the commercialisation phase is where you are using your book as a brand-building, credibility-boosting resource
- **Product extension** – what else can you use your book for, or how else can you share your knowledge? Product extensions include online courses, webinars, retreats, memberships and face-to-face workshops
- **Marketing and (personal) branding strategy** –consider how your book would fit your overall marketing and

personal branding strategy and how you could bring together those important elements of vision, strategy, reader and content to make it marketable. Your market research will inform you of which direction to head in

Is Your Book A Product To Sell, Or Is It Something Bigger?

Slap on your wrist if you say it's a product to sell. Of course, you want it to sell, but your book is bigger than the book. This book is part of your personal branding toolkit. It will help you to open doors and sell other products and services on the back of it. It could be the start of a trend or a cause, and you could create a movement. It is a HUGE business card, a big FAT brochure, but it is never just a BOOK.

Your Product Roadmap

It is worth considering at this stage what else you could create from your book and build in a product roadmap. This is a map of what comes after you have your book. Sometimes you may launch your book with a mini-course (your minimum viable product MVP), followed by a full course, a webinar, retreat and many other products and services. See later for ideas.

Your Unique Planning Process

When I write a book, my planning process starts with going through my plan and putting dates and resources next to each activity. I follow this by sorting my outline with an exercise called

Step it out, which I designed based on NLP timelines. It's a physical walking and brainstorming exercise with post-it notes and voice recording. After SIO, I create a mind map (hand-drawn and on a computer) and then a rough outline in WORD. Once I have an outline, it's on to the chapter framework/format, storyboard, and writing my first chapter.

Without a *process that suits you,* you won't know where and how or why you are travelling in a particular direction. Without *action,* it is unlikely that your book will ever be published.

I get that planning can be a proverbial pain, but it will pay off and right now is a great time to get into the habit of looking at your plan and thinking (and taking action) about what you can do to get you closer to your dream of becoming a published author. Remember to think about the kind of planner you are. Do you love planning, or are you more spontaneous? Then, find planning strategies that work and help you keep up with your plan.

The Potential Cost

Whenever I am asked what is the cost of writing a book, my response is usually, what is the cost of NOT writing your book? Remember (and it certainly feels like it) that it takes approximately 700 hours to produce a non-fiction book. For someone who does it all themselves, a simple calculation will tell you how much it would cost if you paid someone (yourself) by the hour. Go on; multiply your hourly rate by 700, scary, isn't it? *However, as we said, think of the VALUE that the book brings and the other products and services you can create.*

Generally, most authors do not do everything themselves; they will invest in a book coach, editor/proofreader, cover designer, formatter and someone to upload to your online publisher. Your role is to write and edit. That said, I do most of this myself.

I rarely think about the costs of manufacturing a book, as a book for me is an investment in my personal brand and my future. Your 'costed' time and other costs are 'sunk costs'. They are the investment you make to differentiate yourself and your personal brand. Your ideas and unique voice, which lead to your book, are your intellectual property. If done well, your ideas can lead to sustainable growth and future profitability.

Take time to ponder the cost question before considering these three words – cost, price and value.

So, What Is The Cost?

In accounting terms, it is the **cost of producing** something e.g.

Time

Materials

Research and development

Prototyping

Overheads (recurring costs)

Marketing

Any one-off costs

Outsourced items, time, products, manufacturing

From a writer's point of view, the **cost is the amount of money and time spent to produce their book**. Here is the funny (or not so funny) part: if you could sell your books at the production cost, no one would ever buy them – imagine all those hours writing and editing at your hourly rate. So even if you do everything yourself, it is still not FREE because your time is money.

From a reader's point of view, the **cost is the PRICE they are willing to pay**. This is the amount that the author charges plus a markup. The difference is the profit (after your publisher takes their royalties.)

Pricing a book is different from pricing, for example, a computer. There are many factors involved.

What do books in your genre typically sell for?

What is the appetite in your market for books like yours?

Are you well known?

How professional (what is the level of quality, did you get it edited and proofed, etc.) is your book?

As a self-published author, the price you set is **ultimately your choice**. While you want to make a profit, a simple calculation will tell you how many you need to sell to break even and make a profit. Remember, the profit is generally in your add-on products and services.

How To Calculate The Rough Cost

You do all the work yourself – keep a note of all the hours you put in from idea generation, outline, writing, editing, cover design, formatting, uploading, etc. It takes approx. 700 hours to produce a non-fiction book for someone who does it all themselves, so I will use that in the calculations for ease.

If your time cost is £10 per hour – your production cost is £7000

If your time cost is £75 per hour – your production cost is £52,500 (ouch!)

I know that looks scary, so let's be sensible. If everyone used a high figure, books would never get written. However, it is a useful exercise to consider so that you can plan how you will use your book to recoup costs and make a profit from the other products and services that come from your book.

There are, of course, variations on a theme:

- DIY and some outsourcing
- DIY, workshops and some outsourcing
- DIY, workshops and hand-over to professionals who take it to publication
- One-to-one coaching with some of the above

Each of these will reduce your TIME cost and, ultimately, the cost of producing your book (and very likely save your sanity). Therefore, it is more cost-effective and less stressful to get some help!

Cost And Price

You know:

- Cost is what it costs to produce
- Price is what the market will bear for a book from you

Value

The value is what you gain from becoming a published author. The value comes in what a book gives you:

- Brand awareness and visibility
- Credibility
- Profile building
- Platform
- Ability to find and share your voice
- Enables you to shape the future and influence change
- Educate others by reaching out with your knowledge, skills and experience
- Promote yourself more effectively
- Connect to a wider audience
- Build a community, campaign for a cause, and create a different future
- Build your confidence
- Enable collaboration and collaborative thinking
- Personal growth and development
- Motivation and inspiration
- Something that you can use as the foundation to create

other products and services from

The list goes on….

If your dream is to get more clients, have more speaker opportunities, build your brand, and become more successful, a book will help you do that.

If on the back of your book, you could book more clients at a higher price, get more speaker bookings, or sell lots of online courses, the cost of your book would be recouped in no time at all. So, **the cost and price of your book are largely immaterial. Instead, the value of it to you is more important.**

It's good and wise to understand the economics of producing a book. Of course, it is, but ultimately, let me say it again: **the value that YOUR BOOK brings YOU is more meaningful.**

Resources

Along the way, you may need to outsource some of your activities. Here are a few potential partners you may need to support you.

- **Coach** – the person who works with you all the way from idea to publication and often beyond
- **Proofreader** – the person who checks for punctuation, spelling and grammar – always use one
- **Editor** – your copy editor will check for consistency and sense and undertake a deeper review

- **Designer** – the person or team that creates your book cover, images and interior design layout (for both print and digital.)
- **Transcriber** – this is someone who converts your voice recordings into the content. There are online companies that can do this for you. E.g. Rev.com and Otter.ai on your phone
- **Ghostwriter** – Someone who writes some or all of your book for you
- **Printer** – Although you will most likely publish through an online publisher for your print book, you may also want to undertake a more cost-effective print run with a traditional printer (for use at your launch and speaker events). Remember, if you have a traditional publishing contract, you may not be able to do this within the terms of the contract. Check out Vervante.com
- **Launch and other marketing** – It is important that you consider how you will market your book now and start to get the resources in place
- **Website** – If you don't have a website, get one, and if you have one, make space for your book and author profile

You can recruit your support crew from one of the many online sites, such as Fiverr (http://fiverr.com), where you can choose from a vast selection of freelancers with differing prices and abilities. The quality of work on Fiverr has dramatically improved over the years. I have learnt that you need to write a great specification and trial their work.

Why Get A Coach?

It's easy to give up. When alone, we listen to our negative thoughts more than our positive ones. It's not always easy to be our own coach. A good book coach/mentor will keep you motivated and inspire you to take consistent action. When you are stuck or feeling resistance, fed up, or procrastinating, your coach is by your side at the end of the phone or email. Your coach **has the experience and knowledge to know what needs to be done to help you reach your book's publication date.** They will hold you accountable, keep you on track, challenge you, have fun with you, share resources and a whole host of other things, and you would be mad to pay for someone's time and not maximise it.

If your book raises personal issues and upsets, discuss this with your book coach, who may be trained to help you. If not, they can advise you where to get professional help for the area you are struggling with. In cases where there is something personal to be dealt with, I will advise my clients to seek other help to not confuse what we are working on.

Get Yourself A Planning And Writing Buddy

A planning and writing buddy is someone you trust to read your work without judgment, challenge you, and talk through your fears. They may be your best friend, a parent or someone from an online writing community. If you have joined the FaceBook Group (just for support on courses and the book – not for coaching), ask there.

https://www.faceBook.com/groups/thesoulwriterslounge

They don't have to spend lots of time; it could just be something simple like a weekly phone call to ask, "*have you written your next 3000 words, and what help do you need to get through the next 3000?*"

I get that you may not want to share your writing with anyone else, but... Let me share some great reasons why it works and will work for you. First, get rid of your 'fear,' remember *false evidence appearing real*; you do not have a crystal ball, and you do not know what someone else will think. AND remember, all feedback is 'the breakfast of champions.' Listen to what is being said with an open heart, and you will learn a lot, I promise.

Having someone to write with can be lots of fun. Mum and I have what we call write-offs. We pick a subject and just write. Usually, we do what we laughingly call poetry. We don't care; we enjoy it

Having a buddy builds your trust and faith in your writing. Mum and I also chat about our writing because we have absolute trust in each other. We can discuss our hopes, fears, plot lines and motivation.

Someone else can see the lack of flow and inconsistencies. We get too close to our writing, and it all looks great – get over it, no, it doesn't, because we get word blindness

Other people can come up with ideas we never even thought of – thank you so much. This is one of my faves

You get asked good questions, which allows you to reflect – and improve your copy

You will get a better idea of what your reader wants – remember; it's all about the reader, not you

You get an opportunity to help someone else become a better writer

Finding A Writing Buddy

Whom do you know with whom you could share your writing?

Ask them to be your writing buddy

Meet up for coffee or on Zoom

Pick a subject and write

Agree how feedback will be given

Celebrate every success

Actions and Checklist

Remind yourself what your unique planning process is. If you don't have one, create one

Consider the resources you might need

Estimate the cost of the resources

Consider working with a coach

Get yourself a writing buddy

Timings

Once you have worked out your timings and started to write, it may feel like you are in a parallel universe, where time seems to be consumed by your writing. The cleaning gets left. You forget that the world exists outside but be assured that normal life can, and will, resume when the journey is over.

This chapter helps you to focus on how to work out how long it will take you to write your book.

Be Committed

To ensure that your plan comes together, make a commitment, put it up somewhere so you can see it, and it acts as a constant reminder. Remember to move it around, or it will become part of the decoration, and you will forget about it.

My Commitment Statement

On a scale of 0-10, where is your commitment?

I (your name) commit to writing my book (book title) by (date of the first draft)

Next, write whatever POSITIVE statements come to mind that help you to clarify this process

Planning Your Time – Setting Deadlines

If you want to publish your book by a set date, you have to first set your outcome to get it done and then plan your time effectively.

Working Out How Long It Will Take To Write

As with most goals, the end goal – the ultimate prize – often seems daunting and unattainable. However, if you break down an ultimate goal into smaller milestones, your BIG goal suddenly seems within reach.

When writing a book, the idea of writing an ENTIRE book might make you sweat. Most writers will choose a daily or weekly word count to meet deadlines. While there are no hard and fast rules about how long books should be, here are a few general guidelines to consider in setting your writing goals:

- Most short eBooks are about 20,000 words and take a reader 1-2 hours
- Longer non-fiction books are 40,000-60,000 words and take a reader 3-4 hours
- A 'typical' chapter is between 3000 and 5,000 words

A traditional self-published book is anything over 30,000 words. The number of words per page in a print book will differ, as you will be creating a book to a specific page size, e.g. 6x9 rather than A4.

- Imagine your book is 30,000 words
- How many words can you write in an hour? 500 or 1000?
- How many words can you write per day? 1000, 2000 or 3000?
- Will you write every day, or will you set a weekly target?

This is clearly not an exact science, but it will focus your mind on your writing outcomes. If you are the kind of person, who goes into overwhelm when you see big numbers, focus on the small numbers, i.e. the number of words per hour or per day.

Later, you will discover quicker ways to get your first draft written. The process is:-

- First draft (write, don't edit)
- First edit
- Second and third edit
- First print proof (I always do this step, even for a digital book)
- Next edit
- Second print proof (which I share with beta readers and book reviewers)
- Final edit
- Proof-reader
- Last print proof

Reading my book as a 'real' book (printed) helps me see it in another light. Once I have done my final edit, which I call my final proof, I will send it to the proofreader, which normally takes about 2 weeks.

You may additionally send your proof books to beta-readers before the proofreader gets them. Beta-readers are trusted colleagues who will not only review it for you, but they will also point out any errors.

Timed Tests

In your first exercise, you're setting a target deadline for having the first draft of your book complete. To be successful with this project, it's imperative that you set a realistic goal. For example, giving yourself two weeks to write a draft in the middle of the holiday season when you stress out normally about writing a blog post will most likely cause you to throw the computer out the window in despair.

Instead, check your calendar, evaluate how you feel about writing in general (i.e., can you bear to sit at your computer and focus on writing every day?) and build in some extra time in case an emergency arises – or if you have unexpected guests arriving for a long weekend stay.

The second exercise is a writing test. It's a private test to see how fast you can write. There's no passing or failing this test, but it will help you create a realistic timeline for finishing your first draft. First, choose a topic related to your book and write for an hour (without editing). Then, use the "Word Count" feature to determine how many words you can write in an hour.

This last exercise is committing to a daily word count. If you don't see yourself sitting down to write daily, choose a weekly word count instead. Consider your schedule as well as your family obligations. I'm a big fan of time blocking, so block off time on your calendar to write; and make this commitment non-negotiable (which means tell your spouse, partner, family, friends, clients, etc.). I usually write first thing in the morning.

Lastly, celebrate your small wins. Celebrate when the week is over, and you've reached (or surpassed) your word count goal. Celebrate when you finish chapters. Celebrate when you look forward to your writing sessions. You don't need to wait until your book launch to celebrate!

Set A Target Draft For Having Your First Draft Finished

When do you ideally want to have your entire book done? First, choose a launch date, then work backwards – looking at your calendar – and choose a realistic date for finishing your first draft.

First Draft Deadline

- When do I want to LAUNCH my finished book?
- Are there any activities, events, seasonal events, or holidays between now and my launch date?
- Do I have the desire to write daily, or do I want to pick and choose the days I write?
- You will need to make edits. How much time do I need to reread my book, take editing notes, and make changes?
- Estimate how many days you'll need for each task.
    - Reread book
    - Make changes
    - Reread final draft
- Do I have the budget and/or desire to hire an editor and/or proofreader?
- Add extra time for their turnaround
- I COMMIT TO HAVING MY FIRST DRAFT COMPLETED BY

Test How Fast You Write

Write for an hour (without editing) on a topic related to your book. Then, use the Word Count feature to find out how many words you can write in an hour. Next, write for a second hour (it can be on a different day), use the Word Count feature, and then take the average of the two numbers for an accurate estimate.

My Timed Writing Test

Article 1 - Word Count in 1 hour

Article 2 - Word Count in 1 hour

My Writing Average

Article 1 Word Count + Article 2 Word Count =

Total Word Count / 2 articles =

Choose Your Daily Word Count

If a daily word count doesn't make sense for you, choose a weekly word count instead. Then, write it down and commit to it.

- My Average Word Count - Per hour is
- How much time can I commit to writing each day?
    - 1 hour = x words
    - 2 hours = x words
    - 3 hours = x words
- How many days per week do I want to write?

- 1 day = x words
- 2 days = x words
- 3 days = x words
- 4 days = x words
- 5 days = x words
- 6 days = x words
- 7 days = x words

(Take your total from the box above and multiply that by the number of days you want to write, giving you a weekly word count total)

I COMMIT TO WRITING

x words daily OR x words weekly

These tests are designed to help you determine how you work and how long, given the right ingredients, it will take you to write.

The Time Stealer

Working out how long it will all take in a perfect world is all well and good. However, procrastination and time stealers are the enemies of the writer. So, for everyone who hates planning, just swap TV time for writing time. Have a go at working out where your wasted time is. Ask yourself:

How long do I take doing unimportant things that take me away from my writing?

Is there a pattern to my time-wasting activities?

This exercise is great for planners, and even if you hate planning, just try it. It will be interesting to see where you waste or use your time.

Step One – Record It

Record what you do in an activity log, noting the date and time, activity, how long it took, and what value that activity has to your overall day. E.g. Watching Emmerdale (or other fascinating soaps): 30 minutes per day, value – low.

Step Two – Break It Down And Put IT Into Priority Order

Take each activity and break it down into its smallest part and decide where on your urgency scale it is: Important and urgent. Important, not urgent. Not important, but urgent. Not important and not urgent.

Step Three – Your To-Do List

Do your important and urgent first. Now that you can see what you have on your plate, do it now and create some writing time, knowing that the urgent and important things have been tackled. If you put this in Excel, you will be able to sort your tasks by order of urgency and importance. Make your to-do list sexy. Okay, that may be impossible. However, if having a gorgeous iPad with an organisation tool works for you, then use that. Equally, if a pad and pencil are for you, use that. Please embrace and love your very sexy to-do list.

Your Writing Timetable

No two people write the same way, so you need to find a way that works just for you. Whatever that way is, it is perfect. For example, we use a map when we want to go somewhere. Your process is your unique map.

To find out what your map is, it would be useful to understand how another writer writes and notice their patterns. In a perfect world, we should be able to interview, watch and fully understand how an expert writer operates. Sadly, we don't live in an ideal world, and you may not have access to other writers over the weekend – but you could plan for some interview time.

This means you will have to map out what you do and how you do it. Analyse it and work out how you can become more effective and efficient in the process or accept the way in which you do things and make allowances. Remember, you are not alone, and there are always tools, people, and resources you can call on for help.

To work out your process, you must walk through all the steps *you* take.

The key now is to think about how you will get the most value out of your writing process. After I have outlined my book, I start by mapping out what I think I want to write about using a 'what', 'why', 'how' and 'what if' framework (more on that later). Then, I look at keywords, key messages, concepts and calls to action and consider how it fits together and flows.

After a period of reflection, I undertake a knowledge audit, which tells me what I can re-purpose, what needs researching and what I can write straight off. Then it is write, write, write! Followed by periods of editing and more writing. Followed by remapping and reflecting. I am not linear in how I work, and I have to force myself to keep returning to my plan and refocusing. I am extremely good at writing too much and brutal at editing.

Important Factors For Your Writing Timetable To Work

Discipline

You need discipline – full stop. Sometimes it is very difficult to be disciplined and getting on with your plan, writing or editing. The dog needs walking, the kids need feeding, and your clothes need ironing! Look at your writing plan, the number of words you set yourself and the time you allowed. Stick to it, and you will create a habit. When you have created a habit, this will be hard to break. Consider the behavioural patterns that you have, understand yourself and try to flex your style.

Setting Boundaries

Let your important people know that you need time and space to write. Give yourself permission to take the time out to write. When it comes to writing, set a timer so that you write for your optimal period and ensure you take a rest.

Creating The Right Environment For You

Where gives you the most peace to write? If your space is not right, with the best will in the world, writing will become a chore. Turn all the noise off; that means phones, the internet and other distractions. Do you need to go to a coffee shop or sit in a cafe? Is there a space in your home that is just right for you? What about a certain chair or room? Only you will know.

Right Tools

Computer, smartphone, post-it notes, a roll of brown paper (brainstorming, your journal, etc. What do you need? Nothing is more frustrating than discovering that there is no paper or ink in your printer when you need to print and edit.

The Right Frame Of Mind

Your mindset may be fixed with certain beliefs about your ability to write this book. I want you to challenge that fixed system, take a hammer to it and shatter it.

Using the power of positive thought is well documented. Feeling positive about yourself and your book is no different and will result in successful outcomes. Where you focus your thoughts, actions will follow, and consistent actions lead to great habits.

Breathe and meditate. Just let your unconscious mind go free. Settle and ground yourself. Ask yourself, what do you have to do to get into the right frame of mind?

Reflect

Without a doubt, when you get to the end of your first draft, you will need to stop and **leave your work for at least one week**. There will be other times that you need to stop and think. Factor them in. Sometimes procrastination is just the way our brains are saying – 'I've had enough, just for now.' **Stop and reflect often.**

Diary, To-Do List Or Timetable

Where will you record the dates and times for your writing timetable? Using your day-to-day digital diary is great as you have a visual of when and if you can set the alarm as an auditory reminder of when to start. What will work for you? Don't forget your writing buddy, who can call to check that you have done your writing.

Actions and Checklist

Calculate how many words you can write in an hour / a half-day and day

Estimate how many words you will write for this book

Decide on a starting date

Ask what activities get in your way and find strategies to overcome them

Decide when you want to be published

Create a writing timetable

How Will You Publish?

In this chapter, you will explore different publishing options. How to publish is an important question—one that often results in confusion for the self-published author. Mostly it comes down to not knowing how and what it will cost. There are many routes and many flavours because this is an ever-evolving industry. Fortunately for you, there is no one-size-fits-all. You can follow different pathways depending on your needs and the ultimate outcome.

I spend a lot of my time explaining the pros and cons of each path to my clients. You need to review them and decide based on what you are publishing and what you want to do with your book.

Let's look at the options, after which you can do some quick research and make an initial choice. Of course, you can change your mind later.

As An Ebook on Your Website

Typically, you will publish your book as a PDF and either give it away for free or sell it via a shopping cart.

Level of control: You do all the setting up and sorting out

Typical process: You write in WORD and save it as a PDF

Royalties: All yours

Advantages: Least amount of investment. It is easy, and you have greater control than some of the other options

Disadvantages: No professional services available. Yes, you can outsource some of the work, but unlike some of the other options, you would have to go and find suitable resources. You also have to work to publicise the book, and, sadly, this route has the least credibility (unless it is a sprat to catch a mackerel and it is your free list-building give away)

Use this option to create an e-book which is your lead magnet.

In this way, you can give your reader a taste of what is to come.

Self Publish

You put your manuscript onto a self-publishing platform. There are many available.

Level of control: Lots. You create and manage your own accounts

Typical process: You upload your manuscript and cover. They may do technical checks, but they do not check your manuscript editorially. You can buy additional services

Royalties: After their share – all yours. Options differ, so check first

Advantages: Easy to use and cost-effective and over time they add more services which will help you to distribute your books

Disadvantages: Not many as lots of site offer a great range of services

Printer/publisher

You give your manuscript to a printer/publisher. They will take your manuscript, convert it ready for print, and handle your warehousing and distribution. They will also format your manuscript for print and digital and then upload them to online platforms. A great companies to look at are Vervante.com and draft2digital.com.

Level of control: You or they manage your account

Typical process: You hand over your manuscript, and they will offer you a range of services that enables you to get your book published on your chosen platform

Royalties: After their costs and the share from publishing platforms– all yours

Advantages: It makes your life easier, and they take the burden of printing and publishing from you. With some, you can also sell your book from your website

Disadvantages: Negligible. Slightly increased cost, and you need to be able to manage the project on top of everything else that you do

Hybrid Publisher (supported self-publishing)

You place your manuscript with imprints such as Balboa Press (Hay House) or Author Solutions (Penguin). They take your manuscript and, depending on your package, will provide a range of services and publish you.

Level of control: They will manage everything to the publishing stage

Typical process: Depends on them. Typically, they will take your finished manuscript and publish it. They may want to proof or run it through editorial services first.

Royalties: Usually a 50:50 split. Check with the company

Advantages: A possible route to the main publisher. They provide a one-stop solution (at a price) and give you access to other useful tools and communities. In addition, they may offer you marketing services (additional cost)

Disadvantages: No guarantees that the 'main' publisher will see your book. You relinquish control of your book, although you should retain the copyright and be able to publish elsewhere – check because this might not be the case

Please read the fine print. Clients have found with this route that they are not allowed to put their book into other online publisher promotions, for example, and have had other restrictions placed on them

Agent to publisher

This route depends on your agent. They will want a book proposal, or possibly the completed book, and will then find the best publisher for you. Terms will depend on negotiations

Level of control: They will manage everything (look at your T&C's)

Typical process: Depends on the agent

You need to have your manuscript completed, and a book proposal/synopsis package put together – per their instructions

Your manuscript may only need to be at the outline and a few chapters stage. You will need a book proposal/synopsis package put together – per their instructions

Royalties: Depends on your contract

Advantages: Your needs are taken care of. Your manuscript will be improved, and you may get an advance

Disadvantages: It takes lots of time and patience to find an agent. Fewer titles are being published this way, so it is inevitably your longest route to market, and there are no guarantees

Whichever route you take, you will still have to build your platform and be prepared to market and sell your book.

Actions and Checklist

Undertake some online research to get a feel for what is available. Find out what it all costs and factor these in if you can. Otherwise, consider your options, make a choice (for now) and add this to your planner (make a note in your diary to pursue next week)

Ask which your favoured route is and why

Make a list of the additional information that you need

Make sure that you will not be hindered by any restrictions later – read the fine print

Ask how does this affect your plan?

Getting Ideas

In this chapter, we are going to have some fun. You will work through some idea-generating exercises that will help you get some clarity about your book. We do this to be clear about what your book will be about when you come to outlining. This chapter kicks these activities off. So put your plan to one side and get ready to explore.

The Museum Of Your Mind

The memory is remarkable, which encodes, stores, and retrieves our experiences. You may well wonder where and how all that stuff gets stored and why you can easily remember some things and not others. In simple terms, information goes in, and we encode it in such a way that makes sense to us, which is why no two people remember the same event in the same way.

Your memory is a pattern of stored connections. So when we want to retrieve a memory, we are taken along a series of pathways (neural pathways), a bit like following a series of directions to an address, where the experience is retrieved and brought into view.

We have stuff in our short-term memory, the things we are actively thinking about, and in our longer-term memory, which is the stuff parked out of the way for now.

Just as wonderful as memory is, it can let us down and often does so in the most awkward circumstances; you know, those embarrassing moments when you introduce someone whose name you should know, and it just doesn't come out. But, on the other hand, as something is remembered, we unconsciously relive it physically, possibly blushing or smiling.

Think of your mind as a museum, with lots of galleries; some of the old masters, some highlighting different periods or themes, some more abstract and some just fragments of times long ago.

As we get older, we seem to forget more things, which is, according to scientists, all part of natural ageing. Even more, reason to write a book. Writing will undoubtedly get your mental muscles working.

Therefore, I recommend you journal so that you can record your journey from the get-go and record important information which will support your book.

Where Do Ideas Come From?

Ideas are all inside and outside of you; they are everywhere. So the question is, how do ideas come to you? Do they just pop into our minds, or do ideas come as a result of lots of small things happening, which, when a good connection is made, creates a new idea pathway so that a bit more of that idea is known?

Coding Our Experiences And Emotions

In every moment, you consume information through your five (or six) senses. These are laid down in your mind-map using your language and coding structure, waiting to be fertilised with another germ of an idea. All these are waiting to be joined by that one all-important connector, which creates the spark and drives it to the forefront of your mind until you get that "eureka" moment.

Provide yourself with the opportunity to become creative by giving yourself space, people to collaborate with and time to reflect. You will be able to exchange and borrow ideas in order to cultivate new ones. Ideas can be incubated for years but appear in what seems a moment with the right stimulus.

Thoughts and ideas come in through the right brain hemisphere as the big picture. They are filtered into detail in the left hemisphere, with both sides working together to enable us to form relationships. We, as writers, are looking for the 'something' that sparks us up and ignites the journey through the mind to create an inspirational network of new ideas and things to write about.

Space

Finding the right place to write or think in is paramount to creativity. In bed, the lounge, conservatory, your office, in your favourite comfy chair. It is important that you find a space or place where you feel at ease, relaxes you, and provides you with the comfort and space to begin writing.

If writing in bed allows your creativity to flow, then write there. However, if you get disturbed, which may cause frustration and anger, go somewhere else and try to recreate the cosy feelings that your bed does. I write in various places and at different times, not through choice but because I get annoyed and demotivated when I get disturbed. In each location, I make the space work for me.

What else do you need in your space? For example, if you are an auditory person, you may like to have some music on, if you are kinaesthetic, you might like to have beautiful things that you can feel, and if you are visual, you might like to be in a place where you can see lovely things.

You may like other things, for example, burning incense or lighting a scented candle. If you love your food, how about a good cup of tea and some raw chocolates? Take some time out to consider your space, what needs to be there or not, to make it the best writing and creative space for you. What and where would be your perfect space?

Headspace

Space is also giving yourself headspace, finding ways to slow down the hustle and bustle of everyday life and giving yourself time to think. Thinking is good and is a perfect way to generate new ideas. But so is quiet time. When you distract the mind, ideas flow.

People

If ideas come from people, who are the people that you interact with, debate with and can run your current ideas across? Brainstorming is one such activity where you share ideas with others.

A Week Of Observation

When your planning weekend is over, I invite you to spend a week of observation. The key is to notice more of what is happening around you. **Take a pen and noteBook wherever you go, observe, notice and listen.** Whom do you meet, what do they say? What is the colour of the train you catch to work? What is the first thing you smell when you wake up? What sounds are around you as you step out of the house? Count how many trees there are on the way to the local shop.

What about these?

The Conversation In The Pub/Bar/Cafe

We meet people everywhere; in pubs and cafes, on the bus or train. Simple conversations with both friends and strangers will spark your imagination. Clearly, with friends, you can share more intimate details and ask for opinions. Whilst I am not advocating getting trashed, going to the pub/bar/cafe and feeling comfortable with friends is a great way to move ideas around and is fun.

Conversations With Your Coach

If you are working with a coach, their role is to listen and challenge your thinking, which will get the grey matter moving. A coach provides space for you to talk, gain clarity, invite curiosity and gives constructive feedback.

Conversations With God, The Universe, Grace, Higher Self

For *god* read, god, higher self, inner voice, the universe, whatever it means to you. These are the moments when you chat to yourself, asking questions and mulling things over, not the mind chatter that gets in the way of productivity. These are the conversations you have when walking or lying in the bath.

Conversations And Questions

What do you get asked about the most? What do your clients ask you the most? When you are in groups or in general discussion, make a mental note of what you are asked the most frequently. This will give you an idea of what your book idea could be about.

Fads And Trends

Out there are all kinds of fads and trends. I can remember the Rubric's Cube, the Cabbage Patch Doll, Tamagotchi's, Calenetics, and a whole host of other things. Calenetics is a great example of an exercise fad, method, or trend (call it what you will) from the 1990s (I think), which recently popped up on my radar. It looks like it's having a revival. Look backwards as well as forwards in your environmental scan. Could you write a book on how to master XYZ?

What's Hot?

Pop up your scanner and note what is topical and hot. How does that feed your book plan? Look at all the books that have been written as a result of the social media revolution. Think of all the labour-saving devices we have, 101 recipes for the microwave or bread maker.

Who Is Talking?

Who is a hot speaker right now? What are they talking about? To which of the STEEPLE categories do their insights belong? Get a copy of their speeches, study them, look for hooks, or use them as potential interviewees for your book.

STEEPLE

I bet unless you have been on any marketing training, you will be thinking, what on earth is a steeple? Rest assured, it is super helpful. A STEEPLE analysis investigates the important factors that are changing that influence a business from the outside. This could be very relevant to your business. It's something that is rarely considered, but I think it will give you a competitive advantage. Look at it with your overall business in mind. Only do the parts that are relevant and appropriate to you. Then, look at the others to see if anything resonates or could be useful.

- **Social** - relates to changes in wider society, such as changes in lifestyles, e.g. numbers of elderly people, higher rates of obesity, changes in tastes and buying patterns, changes to families and demographic patterns, and increase/decrease in public services, changes in working patterns. It also relates to cultural aspects.

- **Technological** - relates to the application of new inventions (IP) and ideas. You only have to look at the internet and social media sites to see how these can influence the world around you. Ebook readers have revolutionised reading. I'm personally addicted to audio books and listen to books every day. Look around you and think about how people like to access information. This will guide how you deliver what you do.
- **Environment** – relates to green, low carbon issues and impacts of anything environmental.
- **Economic** - relates to changes in the wider economy such as rises (or falls) in living standards or the general level of demand, rises or falls in interest rates, client spending power, trade cycles and trends, international money issues, etc.
- **Political** - e.g. a change in government, or a change in government policy, lobby & pressure group issues.
- **Legal** – relates to current and future legislation, laws relating to industries and countries.
- **Ethical** – relates to what is morally right.

Questions to ask:

- What are the key drivers and trends in your external environment which you could / should be addressing?

- What are the implications for your client? How do they grow, change or develop with your insights?

When you have completed, the relevant areas ask: -

- What are the main developments with respect to demographics, economy, technology, government and culture that will/could affect your business and the position it takes in the marketplace?

Social Media

Do you Tweet, FaceBook, YouTube, TikTok, Instagram, Pinterest, or use LinkedIn or any number of social media sites; what is trending? What are people talking about? Twitter's home page lists what's trending and what questions people are asking. What's happening in your groups? What about question and answer sites like Quora? Set up some Google alerts around your topics and see what others are saying.

Plane, Train And Fast Car

When you travel, what can you pick up about trends, forecasts and issues in other countries? Broaden your horizon in your environmental scan. Could you compare the legal or cultural systems, for example, in the UK, US and Africa?

Tune In To The Radio And TV

What is causing controversy or dominating the news? I get media shut down and can't bear to hear the same old story repeatedly. However, guess what? It's hot, relevant and news. So what can you tune into that is relevant to your reader that would make a great book to build your brand?

Subscribe To A Newsfeed Or Newspaper

You can get alerts sent to your email address for many different keywords. Make a point to read what comes through; it will help with ideas and research.

The Market For Writers

When you scan your environment, look at what the media are asking for. On Twitter, you can use the hashtags #journorequest or #prrequest. What are the publishers and agents still open for business on? Which blogs are hot and looking for content? Google 'writers market' and see what comes up. Check out the best-sellers lists (http://www.nytimes.com/best-sellers-books).

Reflection

Reflection is consciously considering our thoughts, experiences, actions and ideas. It is about stepping back and pausing so that you can see, hear and feel. The reflective practice includes some great resources, such as my journal. You will start noticing things you may not otherwise have noticed. This then helps with idea generation. Reflect often.

Record And Reflect

One of the most powerful ways I have found is to talk it through.

All you need is your smartphone. Walk up and down your brainstorming wall and talk about what you see, what ideas pop out, and what aha's you get. Then, listen back, make notes and reflect.

What Is Your One Thing?

What is your one thing? Quite simply, your one thing is the book that you are creating. From that one thing, you can create many things, and as a part of this process, I'd like you to think about the many things you can turn this book into.

Your book, as I keep saying, is not just a book. It will become a part of a much bigger personal branding toolkit. This is the starting point of leveraging your knowledge, skills and experiences. From your book, you can build a business.

Actions and Checklist

Choose the perfect place to create your book ideas project

Spend some time mulling over your book ideas and keep writing ideas down

Keep reflecting and adding more things as they pop up

Consider and reflect on how the ideas that you had thought of initially might have changed (if at all)

Also, add in chapter ideas and anything else that comes to mind

Consider how to turn your one thing into many things

What Is Your Story?

In this chapter, you will look at your history because you are more than a timeline of events. You have a story rich in challenges, lessons and gifts you can be proud of. It is because of your story that you are who you are.

You have overcome challenges, made the most of the opportunities presented, and have arrived here by understanding why obstacles have occurred.

It's time to consider how your story will support your book idea.

Your story is a funny old sausage. I remember sitting in a pub saying to my friends that I was going to become a politician and the CEO of a global company, and I was going to change the world.

I became neither and lost my way because of the things I needed to heal. I was angry at the world because of early abuse and did things to drown the pain out. While I abused my body and chose unhealthy relationships, a part of me wanted so much more, and I needed to prove I had value. This led me to take an MBA (after getting expelled from school) and doing an ILM (institute Of Leadership And Management) Level 7 Executive Coaching Certificate, simultaneously training as an NLP practitioner. And I almost did two more master's degrees to prove I was intelligent.

It took a cruel and narcissistic man to show me the way out. I caught him at something, and that day everything fell apart, but it also gave me the key to finding myself. Putting my two dogs in our motorhome, I drove to another country and fell to pieces while pretending I was ok. In falling apart, I learned to love myself – which was a good job because I had illness after illness. If we suppress our emotions, I believe they will one day find a way out, and mine certainly did.

I healed an overactive thyroid, a fractured spine (with many other complications), shingles, and a fractured rib with a nasty chest infection naturally. When any specialist told me to take drugs, my wild inner child and my bloody-minded older self decided my way or the highway. Boy, oh boy, did I learn a lot about nutrition, the body and energy healing.

But here's the thing even though I wrote endless blogs and a book on healing osteoporosis, it left me cold. Healing was a passion. Nutrition was a passion. Energy medicine, crystals and chakras are a passion. But I was not passionate enough for this to be my calling. I do, however, love to teach these things.

I'd always written; my journal was where I poured my life and my stories. It was there when no one else was. My journal saved my life. Through my own stories and healing, I realised that there was always something that we mere mortals had come to planet Earth to do. All of us have a mission. Mine, it turns out, is not natural healing but to help others heal through writing and using their stories to change the world.

What does that even mean, you may ask? I believe that when you wake up to your story and heal whatever you need to heal, you will find something that calls you. The call of this wild thing will be so strong that you cannot stop it.

One of my clients could live a life of Riley, indulging in her whims. Instead, she has been called to change the world and end human trafficking. She has written a book. While doing that, she planned out a program for schools and collaborations with corporate businesses. Her signature blueprint is a program in schools, which she will use to inspire young people to follow their dreams, be happy, and be who they are. Can you imagine what other possibilities are available to this amazing person? I can.

Another client has a successful membership program and wanted a book to build her brand and enrol more people on her membership. But not only that, she has been called to change the face of therapy and how counsellors are seen. That is a massive undertaking that sits in her heart and soul.

Another client focuses on helping people sleep so they can function in the world. Another helps disillusioned CEOs find a life of fulfilment. Another wants people to be size happy and healthy rather than torture themselves with diets and destructive ways of eating. Another has a way to help her clients overcome IBS. Another is teaching people to move from 3D living to 5D with the assistance of animals.

You see, each of these has experienced something in their lives that has spoken to a deeper part of them, and this right now story is a part of their mission on Earth. Each knows that, like me, they are here to do ONE thing despite the many other things they could teach.

So what is it you have come to Earth to do?

I realise this is a big question, so let's go on an adventure, shall we and explore? Later there will be more questions to continue the process.

Are you ready to explore further? For this adventure through life, there will have been many experiences that have shaped you. Let's uncover them and see what we can glean from them. This is one of my favourite exercises, and I learn something new each time I do it. This will give you the story, lots of stories to share for learning points and for marketing. It is very revealing.

Timelines And Turning Points

The timelines and turning points exercise is a perfect place to begin the journey to uncovering your memories and stories. We use timelines and turning points to help us examine the past. We are looking for clues and connections to possibilities and opportunities that might not otherwise seem obvious. Timelines help us discover your locked away thoughts, memories, skills, talents, and experiences, making up your stories.

Their value comes from **observing and reflecting** on what has been captured on your visual storyboard. When you stand back and observe your life, you will gain a lot of clarity. However, you also need to be prepared to keep walking away to reflect, coming back and trying to see what is missing or what needs moving around. You are looking for patterns, connections, and themes.

Why Timelines Are So Powerful

Timelines are powerful because they are a storyboard, a pictorial representation, and humans see things in patterns. It really is as simple as that. The powerful part comes in taking time to stand back and reflect. Let your unconscious mind go into flow and make the connections. When you do this using visually using colour, your story comes alive.

So even if you are a person who says I am a logical left-brainer, let me stop you. You have two sides of your brain. Regardless of how you want to pigeonhole yourself as a 'list kind of person', your brain will do what it wants. It will use all of its processing power on the right side for the big picture and the left for detail and connections. This exercise will enable you to uncover the book of your life, so hold that in your intention.

How To Create A Timeline

Start Brainstorming

- Get a large sheet of paper
- You are going to create a timeline across the top in blocks and themes (life areas) along one side
- Armed with post-it notes of a variety of colours and coloured pens/pencils, put your date of birth at one end and today's date at the far end
- Next, divide your timeline into blocks of seven years
- Along the side, put in these life areas (you can use others)-
    - Health and wellbeing
    - Learning
    - Financial
    - Heart and spirit
    - Experiences
    - Mental/emotional
    - Love/Partner
    - Family
    - Friends
    - Mission/Vision
- Start brainstorming

- As you look at the themes and time zones, let thoughts come into your mind without censorship
- As a thought comes to mind, put it on a post-it and place it where you consider it should go for now. You might use similar colours for certain thoughts or ideas
- When you have brainstormed, take some time out
- Later reflect on what you have written, move things around and add more, do not get rid of anything
- When you are ready, start looking for connections, themes and aha moments
- Consider how your developmental years have impacted your personal growth
- Use coloured pens to mark up how each experience maps to your life now
- Use your journal to write about what comes up

Once you can see the connections, you will be able to see where your life themes are. For example, things that happened in childhood may have created a lack of self-worth as an adult, which has meant that you have always settled for mediocre jobs rather than becoming an entrepreneur. Health issues could directly result from emotional pain from actions or inactions. Poor relationships may be a relentless search for someone like (or unlike) your father. Your inability to write and publish a book could be linked to self-worth around being told you were a rubbish speller.

Once you have completed your timelines exercise, you are ready for turning points.

Turning Points

This is another exercise I like to do with lots of reflection. Please take your time. What will happen is that once you have started, your unconscious mind will continue in its flow state and keep throwing things at you.

Examining the past can be upsetting, especially when you look back and see a set of repeated behaviours that might now seem cringeworthy. However, I like to think that despite everything that has happened, it was all meant to be and is just part of the journey, like a tough degree programme at the University of Life. Everything is a learning experience, with challenges, lessons and gifts.

- Go back to your timeline and start looking for turning points
- Make a note of each of these, ensuring that they stand out

Next, take each of your turning points and do the following:

- Using your journal, create a page (or two) for every turning point
- On each sheet, answer the turning point questions below; you can add your own, but for now, let's keep it simple
- Look for points at which you changed direction or made important, potentially life-changing decisions or points at which change was thrust on you

- Look for times of personal and spiritual growth
- Look for ideas that could help you create the journey map for your story – the one that you take your clients on

Turning Point Questions

- Describe your life at this time?
- What did you learn that contributed to your spiritual and personal growth?
- What were the challenges, lessons and gifts?
- How have these empowered you to be a better person, and how have these helped you to help others?
- What are you grateful for learning about?

Your Life File

You will have a 'life' file at the end of the writing period. This file is useful for when you feel stuck in the creation process. When you understand what got you here, good and not so good, you have the knowledge to support you moving forward with your book.

Focus On The Gifts

Did you look for your gifts? There are gifts in all of these situations. If my first husband hadn't told me I was stupid, I wouldn't have done an MBA. If I hadn't have left him and been with my next partner for sixteen years, I wouldn't have had many great memories, learned to ride a motorbike and discovered fine wines and when we broke up, have the cash to buy my current home, even if it was a wreck. If the last husband hadn't been discovered living a highly promiscuous double life, I wouldn't be living in my lovely home in the peace of the hills with my dogs. I wouldn't have my first two dogs if he hadn't wanted a dog. If I hadn't felt suppressed in a male-dominated environment, I wouldn't have taken the ILM Level 7 Executive Coaching qualification, which has helped me with my coaching career. If I hadn't gone through a series of illnesses and healed myself naturally using nutrition and energy medicine, I wouldn't be able to maintain my energy to support others. If writing hadn't been my saviour, I would be helping people discover who they are and how their stories can help heal the world.

Your gifts are part of your story and journey, and you can use yours to teach others how to find their gifts and heal with your insight, knowledge, skills and your process.

We know so much more than we give ourselves credit for, often to our detriment. Ask yourself, how did you manage to get where you are today? That's right; you applied lots of your experience, skills, and knowledge. Your skills might include:-

- **Communication** – the way in which you speak with your friends and family or show how you feel
- **Teamwork** – the way in which you are ready to muck in and work in collaboration with others
- **Leadership** – the way in which you motivate and encourage others while taking the lead

- **Initiative** – the way in which you spot opportunities, set and achieve goals
- **Solving problems** – your logical or creative thinking which helps you to find solutions to problems
- **Flexibility and adaptability** – the way in which you have adapted to new situations – what about that time you were chucked into the deep end of a situation, and you just got on with it?
- **Self-awareness** – knowing your strengths and having the confidence to use them
- **Commitment and motivation** – just getting on with what's needed
- **Finance** – being able to balance the books – paying the bills, saving for nice things, sorting out your credit cards
- **Inspiration** – inspiring others to know what is possible
- **Impact** – impacting other's lives so that they can change, heal and grow and go out into the world to do the same if they so desire
- What else?

There are so many fantastic themes you will discover when you do this. Find them, acknowledge and celebrate them. You are an incredible person. Then ask how you will use what you learn going forward?

You Are The Expert

Not only do stories and themes emerge, but your many talents.

This will help you determine what you can use and what you will outsource to other people.

- Make a list of things you are knowledgeable about
- Write up your most valuable experiences
- Evaluate your skills and talents and determine where you are on a scale of one to ten
- If you are not a ten, what has to happen to get you to a ten? Do you even want to be a ten?
- Now that you have a list of your skills and talents write a short bio about yourself
- How could you apply these skills to this project?
- How could you apply these skills to changing the world – your way?

What Is The Story, And Why?

You may have already known your story and what you want to inspire others with; it may not have been ultra-clear, or you may have had a vague idea; my hope is you can see your story and other stories you can share.

There you have it. We all have a story. What is your story? Then consider why this story? My advice is to journal, reflect, and let the ideas come when you walk, sleep, daydream, or do other unrelated tasks. We are going to explore more later.

Storytelling

Telling stories is not new. People have always told 'tales' because that is how humans make meaning. Not only do you want to use your story as the way you support your clients, but you also want to use your stories to make an emotional connection. Learn how to turn your experiences into fantastic stories that touch other's emotions will move people to connect and take action to work with you. When you tell stories, you will be creating a unique impression where all of your experiences that are woven through who you are will become apparent. Make a list of your stories and ask:-

- What was the challenge or issue?
- What was the outcome?
- What stories can you tell to show off a product/service where you have already delivered great value and experience?
- What is the point of each story, and why is it a good point?
- Make a list of all of your products and services case studies or testimonials, and find the stories

When you have your stories mapped out, write them up and practice telling them. You could do this to video and then use that content for your blogs, your YouTube channel, and any online courses or programs you create. Even if you are not ready to do this bit, start a file and collate them for later.

Actions and Checklist

What does your timeline bring up for you?

What do you see as your gifts?

What themes are appearing for you?

What amazing skills or talents do you have?

What are your stories that are worth sharing?

What is the story that you will share with the world?

Getting Clear – Values To Vision

In this chapter, we are going on a journey from values to creating a vision. This will provide even more clarity around – is this the right book for right now?

I believe it is important to understand who you are, your values, passion, purpose, and vision and use them as a starting point for discovering your book. I also think that knowing where you are, where you want to go, and what you want to create is equally important. So let's start with that and then move on to you.

Knowing who you are and what wonderful things you have to pass on makes it easier to start and continue to write. Being clear about who you are and what you stand for will give you a baseline for this book. In this chapter, you will start to get closer to what your book might be about.

Where Are You?

Put A Stake In The Ground And Look Around

This may seem very simple, but it is, in fact, very powerful and may bring up all kinds of feelings. It is important that you look around you and take it all in. Although we are creating and writing a book, you may find that other things are creeping in. That is ok. Write all your reflections in your journal and do not analyse them. Simply acknowledge that this is where you find yourself. Describe where you find yourself. Consider how this feels. What do you see, and what do you know about this place?

Where Do You Want To Go?

Thinking about where you want to go tells your imagination to start getting creative, and you will start to see signs everywhere.

So make a note of these, no matter how odd they may seem at the moment.

Go sounds like a destination, and you may know where and what this destination looks and feels like. But, equally, you may not.

What Do You Want To Create?

Creation is about envisioning, and it might mean mission to you. Often if you can't see it, you can't create it. For example, you may have already written down some of what you want to create, but you might not have realised it.

Where you want to go and what you want to create require you to think of an endpoint, not the final destination. In his famous book, Covey talks about starting with the end in mind. What is this end? You may want to write a book that helps you create a business.

The key is to make a start and then amend as you learn more about your desires, goals and intentions.

Your Purpose-Led Book

A purpose-led book is an intrinsic part of you and what you have to impart. It will have been written from your heart so that you can connect to other hearts. It is also a book that can serve a bigger purpose. Getting from values to vision is a process which steps you through values, passion, purpose and vision.

Taking steps through the process and working out your values and passion leads you toward your vision. Without a vision, you do not have a direction. Without direction, you cannot take meaningful and purposeful steps.

The way I see it is that our essential truths – our values (beliefs) – ignite the fire in our bellies and are what drives us as humans.

Passions are what keep the fire burning. When you connect these, you can create a vision for the future, which will light your path and drive the direction towards your purpose, big why and mission. When you have **clarity**, you can define where you are heading.

VALUES + PASSION = your WHY (purpose) and WHAT (fulfilling that purpose)

WHY **inspires** your VISION

WHY = the **driving force** in your WHAT

VISION **stimulates and helps to create** GOALS, ACTION and a sense of PURPOSE

A sense of PURPOSE **drives** your HOW

Only when you know your WHY and can communicate it can you inspire others. Your WHY is rooted in knowing who you are. Everything you have ever done, all your experiences, creates your core values and beliefs; it is essentially WHO you are and what INSPIRES you. It is from your passion that you do WHAT you do; it is the heart and soul of an authentic brand, where your WHY, WHAT and HOW you do IT are all in balance and perfectly aligned. People work with you based on an emotional connection to your 'why' when they feel and read your passion. That's when they are inspired.

By walking through the process, you will be led toward your vision. Without a vision, you do not have a clear way forward. So kick off your shoes, pull up a chair and let's explore.

When we have **clarity,** we can define where we are heading with our writing. In finding out about ourselves, we start to **gain clarity of purpose**. What you are passionate about and the purpose of your writing go hand in hand. Your readers will have expectations. Your role as a writer is to make sure those expectations are met while at the same time fulfilling the purpose of your writing.

Your Perfect Day

This powerful exercise engages your subconscious mind and sets a detailed blueprint of your life using the power of focused visualisation. In this exercise, you're going to imagine your perfect day. So give yourself permission to let your imagination go wild with this one. Make it as far out and as wonderful as your wildest dreams.

Getting fully involved in the imagining with this exercise will open up your creativity, and you'll be surprised at the things you will learn about yourself.

Part 1

Take a pen and paper, find somewhere quiet and answer the following questions. It's important to answer them in the present tense as if you are currently experiencing them and be as accurate and detailed as possible. Really let your imagination run away with you but try to keep an element of realism.

Some people might find it easy to imagine a million-dollar house. In contrast, others will find it difficult to imagine more than a small apartment. It doesn't matter. Just do what's comfortable while still thinking as big as you can. And remember, you can always do this again at a later date. Don't worry if the exercise takes several attempts to finish; just be sure the answers are truly what you want. **Ready, here goes...**(remember to write your answers down)

Where do you live?

- Be precise
- The country right down to the street you live in
- What do you see, feel, and sense when you stand outside your home?

Describe your house/home

- What does it look like?
- Describe your furniture
- Describe the energy of your home
- What do the fixtures and fittings feel like?

- What colours do you use?
- What sounds can you hear?
- What does it smell like?
- How do you feel about it?

Describe your car

- Maybe you have several cars?
- Describe the exact make, model and colour
- Take your car for a test drive. How does it feel?

Work

- What would your business be?
- What time would you start work?
- What would you actually do at work?
- What are your clients like?
- How do you help your clients to transform?
- How do you inspire and impact others' lives?
- How do you do what you do?
- What do you love most about the work that you do?

Leisure time

- What do you do for exercise?
- What hobbies, sports, or pastimes do you enjoy?
- What do you do for personal fulfilment?

Family

- Do you have a spouse or partner?
- Do you have children?
- Describe your family
- What do you do for family time?

Holidays/vacations

- What kind of holidays/vacations do you take?
- How many holidays/vacations do you take?

Health

- What is your health like?
- What have you healed?
- Describe your diet and the foods you love to eat
- How often do you do exercises?
- What type of exercises do you do?

Sleep

- Describe your bedroom
- What do the sheets and mattress feel like?
- What time do you usually go to bed?
- How many hours of good quality sleep do you get?
- What time do you usually wake up?

Describe your perfect morning

- What can you feel, hear, see, and smell when you wake up?
- What do you have for breakfast, and where do you have it?
- Who are you eating with?
- What is your morning routine?
- Why does your routine work so well for you?

Lunch

- What food do you have for lunch?
- Describe the tastes and smells
- Who are you eating with?
- Do you have lunch with friends?
- What are your friends like?
- What do you talk about?

Dinner

- Where do you eat?
- Describe the food, including colours, textures, smell and taste
- Who do you eat with?
- What do you talk about?

Evening Time

- What do you do in the evening?
- Do you read, watch TV or a film/movie, or walk on the beach?
- How do you end your day?

There, that wasn't so hard, was it? That little exercise can produce astounding results! It tells your unconscious mind exactly what you want out of life and gives you an insight into what's really important to you. I first did this exercise about five years ago. Like many people, I did it for fun without believing it would make a difference. I re-discovered my scribbles a few years later and was stunned to see that I had virtually everything on it. Some of the things had turned out a little differently, but the core of each item had been realised.

Part 2

Now that you've completed part 1 of the exercise, you will use your notes to write your own story. Just put pen to paper and scribble. For example, you could start something like this:

"I live in a beautiful traditional house in the countryside in Spain, nestled in the hills, overlooking the sea. I am woken every day at 6:30am by the sounds of birds in the garden and the sun streaming through my bedroom window...."

And carry on from there.

Ideally, you should write this by hand, but please print it out if you write on a computer!

Part 3

Now for the really exciting bit.

Bringing it alive

- Create a scene in your mind of an imaginary movie theatre. Imagine yourself sitting in the centre of the front row
- In front of you is a large screen, and on it is the start of your perfect day story
- Start the movie and run your story all the way to the end
- At the end of the movie, freeze the last frame
- Turn up the colours, the brightness and the sounds and imagine yourself walking into the movie on the screen
- Fully absorb yourself into the "you" on the screen
- Restart the movie and become the star of your perfect day
- Run the movie several times at normal speed while experiencing all of the wonderful colours, sounds and experiences of the new you. See the sights, hear the sounds and feel the feelings
- Then freeze the last frame
- Repeat the process until this feels real and exciting

This technique lets your unconscious mind know that this is your reality and will now conspire with you to make everything in the movie happen. Read through your perfect day often and run the visualisation exercise several times. Muse on this as you go about your day. You can even do this as part of your daily meditation or walk. And don't forget to watch for the changes that show up in your life and record these in your journal.

Part 4

Create a mini vision board, and add pictures and affirmations that represent your perfect day.

Part 5

Finally, plant your perfect day in a small plant pot or perhaps a candle holder, and add things that feel enriching. I, for example, would add crystals; you could add hearts and light a candle. If you have an altar, put your pot on there. And, once you set out a clear description of your perfect day and focus on it often, your unconscious mind will do everything it can to balance out the reality it sees with the reality it has been shown. Once you have the story of your perfect day set in stone, you can help support it by bringing it to mind often.

Values

Values are ways of being that mean something important to you. Your values are the qualities that you want to present to the world. They are what you believe is important. They are the foundations of who you are.

Values are those things that you come back to, which tell you that your life is going in the right direction. The number that you have are not relevant. What is important is that you know what they are. They can change as your life changes.

What is interesting about exploring values for a book project is that you will see your values being expressed in all parts of it and how you bring them to market.

Discovering Your Values

Once you are clear on your values, you can move towards them. Once your mind can visualise them, and you believe them, your mind, being very clever, will just know what they are. Using a book to build your business is a very values led activity. If what you create does not fit with your values, chances are you will not do it.

Discovering Your Values From Your Perfect Day

Go back to your perfect day and look for value words. What I mean by this is, look for words that stand out in what you have written. These could be: -

Abundance, acceptance, balance, beauty, creativity, calm, determination, difference, energy, empathy, freedom, focus, generosity, grace, happiness, heart, ingenuity, impact, joy, justice, kindness, knowledge, love, loyalty, mastery, modesty, navigate, network, open, outrageous, peace, passion, quirky, quick, respect, recognition, safe, spiritual, tradition, tranquil, unique, understanding, vision, vitality, worldly, wise, young, zeal, zip.

- You will know which words your value words are.
- When you have your list of value words, put an X next to the ones that resonate, the key is not to think too much and go with your gut
- Cut that list down to just six or eight words
- Then put them in order of importance to you
- It is perfectly natural to be surprised when you see the words; conversely, there may be nothing new for you

Discovering Your Values #2

This is another values exercise that will help you gain clarity. When you have done this one, compare your two lists and come up with a definitive five.

- Write out 30 words that mean something to you. Do this quickly
- It may make it easier to use post-it notes and a wall
- Once you have 30 words, start to group like words together
- Start choosing your eight; you will, I am sure, have more
- Next, be brutal and whittle your list down to just eight
- Put your eight values to one side
- Keep the other words safe as you may find that you will want to use them for another purpose
- Compare this list with your first list and choose just five

When you understand your values, you can use them to decide

how to live your life AND how you will express them in your book and personal branding. Staying connected with your values is an ongoing lifetime activity. Take the time to understand your values and the real priorities in your life; from there, you can set your direction and stick to what you believe in and are passionate about. These values will shine through your voice and inspirational message – in your book.

You will then be able to answer questions such as:

- What value will my reader get from my book?
- What value will I get from writing my book?
- What business should I be in?
- What career path should I pursue?
- Should I start my own business?
- What compromises am I willing to make?
- Should I follow what others expect or go with my heart?
- What books should I write?
- Will my books be about what's important to me or what I do (is that the same thing?)

Values And Why

Do one final check that your five values resonate with you

Next, to each value, write about why it is important to you

Passion

Your passion, combined with your knowledge and skills, is what you will be distilling through your writing. You may be passionate about many things. We are looking for the one thing you could write about that resonates with you right now.

Finding Your Passion

People often talk about finding their passion or writing about what they are passionate about. So, what is passion to you? For me, it's doing the things I want to do, doing the things I love, and find easy, and doing the things that give me the greatest pleasure.

Notice I use the words "the things". You can be passionate about many things, which is often the issue; which passion is THE PASSION? Passion is very rarely about one thing; there will be a whole range of things that you absolutely adore doing. When you answer these questions, it will become clearer: -

What are you good at, or have a natural aptitude for, that you love doing? *Not "what are you good at but hate"*. Sometimes we get caught up being an expert at something and somehow tell ourselves because it is easy, and we do it well, that it is a passion – it is not

- What do you NOT like doing?
- What do you choose to do?
- What would you choose not to do?
- When you were a child, what did you love to do?
- When you lose track of time, what are you doing?
- Who or what are you envious of? Why?

- Think back to the last time someone said your eyes lit up when you were talking. What were you talking about?
- What would be on your list if everything you were passionate about was taken away, and you only had 30 seconds to make a list?
- If nothing were standing in your way, what would you be doing?
- If money were no object, what would you do every day?

- What would you learn if you could learn anything and it was fun?
- Who or what inspires you?
- What do you research the most when sitting in front of your computer?
- Imagine you are sitting with a friend. What do you talk about the most – what lights you up?
- Look at your bookcase. Which books interest you the most?
- What problems do others face that you find easy to sort out?
- If you had a gift for the world, what would it be?
- What is your inspirational message for the world?

Review the answers to these questions and write your perfect day story again. When you have completed that, reflect and write the answer to this question. What I am passionate about is…

Test It

Take yourself back through the last hour, day, week, month or year and consider the following:

- What choices do I consciously make that move me closer to what I love doing?
- Conversely, what choices don't I make?
- Is what I am, or have been, doing bringing me closer to what I love doing or further away?
- Do I feel energised and engaged in my job?
- Do I feel lucky to be paid to have this much fun?
- Would I still do the work I am doing now, even if I did not need to work?
- Look in the mirror and ask, "What have I done today that energises me? What and who do I see looking back at me?"
- Ask others to describe you and your personal brand.

Use these questions to ask trusted colleagues and friends what they think. Pull out the salient points, the repeated words or phrases, and look for commonality and difference. What does this tell you?

Vision

Vision drives your direction; it is future-based and relies on taking action to get you there. Your vision, then, is something that will propel you towards things that you want to achieve in the future. Your personal vision statement is a **written description of your future desired life** as seen in your mind's eye. There is no right format or length. However, the more detailed and specific your vision is, the more connected to you it will be and the easier it will be to set your outcomes or goals.

A personal vision is based on your emotional aspirations, representing a picture of the future – *your future*. The difficulty is that we do not have full control of the future. This means that your vision can often creep from being something that is galvanising and motivational to an aspirational picture that is sketchy and difficult to achieve. The challenge is to identify how to convert the aspiration into reality.

Craft Your Vision Statement

Reflect on your values and passion, think about who you are, where you want to be, what you want to create and what you want to be known for, and then design a meaningful statement.

Write in the first person and make your statement about the future you want

- Be specific about what you want to achieve
- Set a time frame
- Articulate the statement in such a way that it can be evaluated and measured

Ask the questions:

- What are my critical success factors?

- Does this vision challenge me?
- What will I have if I achieve it?
- What will I have if I don't achieve it?
- What won't I have if I achieve it?
- What won't I have if I don't achieve it?
- What am I prepared to invest to realise this vision?

Walk Towards Your Vision

I'm a great fan of vision boards and having them where you can see them. But more importantly, placed where you can walk towards them. In my office, my vision board is in front of my desk. The vision board is not static because as I stand and muse over it, I find something I may want to add.

You can do the same with your book vision. Create a vision board with things like the title, ideal reader, a cover mock-up of what your book will give you, as well as other things that are meaningful to you.

Have fun creating a vision board for your book, brand and business. Place it where you 'have' to walk towards it every day.

My Future Self Looking Back

I find it helpful to write a story about my future self. I date and time the story and write as if I were looking backwards to today. I write about my achievements and how I arrived at this point. This is a great trick for the mind; it will believe you and ensure you achieve it. Do this twice, once for your personal vision and once for the vision for this book.

Purpose

Purpose means intention; for example, you eat healthy food with the intention of nourishing yourself and preventing dis-ease. You use your eyes with the intended purpose of seeing things, possibly looking out for beauty or danger; your heart's purpose is to pump blood amongst other things, and with your ears, you hear and listen. Products have a purpose. A pen's purpose, for example, is to enable you to write and communicate through the words you write. The pen is created with a purpose, and its user uses it for that purpose. People can walk purposefully, behave purposefully, and act with determination and purpose. Occasions can have a purpose; for example, a charity event's purpose is to raise money.

Something that has a purpose has a use or can be used as intended by its creator

Your values, passion and vision combined give you some aims and goals – something to drive you onwards. This **sense of purpose** keeps you heading in the right direction towards what you want – sharing your vision and message. Having a sense of purpose means doing something meaningful to you. Your sense of purpose is inspirational and motivational. It provides the drive you need to overcome anything that gets in the way of writing your book.

Life purpose is what you are meant to experience in this life.

These are your life's lessons, the ups and downs, the 'stuff' you encounter to discover your message and why you are here. For me, given the lack of concrete facts, my belief system tells me that life purpose is a journey and the lessons we agreed to learn in this lifetime. I believe that life purpose is based on themes such as love, loss, happiness, tragedy, forgiveness, letting go, overcoming ego, wealth, debt, and causes, such as people, the planet, animals and poverty.

These lessons come in small bursts and will continue until the lesson is learnt. Think about how tedious it is to keep on dating rubbish men or women, or meeting other kinds of toxic people, or feeling ill because of the processed food you shovel down your throat. You will invariably be shown your lessons until you embrace and learn from them. These make fantastic themes for books.

Common purpose is shared purpose, where your community, tribe or soul group share your themes, causes and passions. Birds of a feather flock together.

Soul purpose is multi-faceted. I believe we are here to:

- Experience human life
- Reconnect to why we are here
- Live a purposeful life
- Share our message (one way is via a book)
- Fulfil our destiny
- Make the most of this journey back to the light

Soul purpose is discovered, not created, and is your BIG 'WHY.'

Purpose, a sense of purpose, life purpose, common purpose and soul purpose are all about 'why'. Each one is interrelated and builds on one another. Our purpose drives us, gets us up each day, and is our mission in life.

Your writing will flow when you write with purpose; you will feel a deep connection to it.

The purpose of your book is to help others imagine **what is possible for them** from what you have discovered, experienced, learnt and are now sharing. By knowing your values and IKIGAI, you are a step closer to knowing your purpose and the book's purpose. Linking your passions to opportunities will help you to tune into those possibilities.

When your purpose is discovered, everything feels like it flows, and you will feel a deep connection to it. Purpose gives you the force and energy to mobilise you towards your vision. A strong sense of purpose motivates you to act.

Writing about subjects that fire you up and align with your values, passion, vision, and purpose is so much more fun than dreary ones that leave you cold and unmotivated. And why would you write a book that doesn't come from your heart?

Finding your purpose leads to a purposeful book or one with a purpose. A purpose-led book is written from your heart; it has meaning to you and those you share it with. For example, all organisations have a mission statement driven by their values and how they conduct their business. As individuals, we call it a purpose statement.

Ikigai

Another way to look at the passion and purpose question is to consider finding your IKIGAI. Ikigai roughly translates into the meaning of your life. It is useful because it wakes you up to your reason for being and helps you live a life where you feel fulfilled. I believe that the books we write must both speak to our hearts and be commercially viable.

The basis of IKIGAI is not to only enrich your own life but also to enhance the lives of others

Every person has a strong drive to find meaning in life – purpose.

They have intrinsic motivation and are seeking fulfilment and inner peace.

Purpose and meaning arrive at different times of your life, which means you can have as many IKIGAI's as you like. Defining your Ikigai is a very personal and private journey. However, combining it with some proactive business planning can result in achieving what you dream about and much, much more!

For me, this is about finding your one thing. When someone comes to write a book, they may find their lives disrupted as they work through their process and identity, getting the book out into the book. They start with 'just' a book idea, then realise it's more than the book. It's their brand and their business.

Four Questions

There are four important questions I'd like you to consider.

What do you LOVE?

What are you GOOD at?

What does the world NEED?

What can you be PAID for?

These four questions are fundamental to working out your book idea and the business you want to create around it. Please take your time and spend time reflecting on each area. Then notice where you feel the excitement and where you feel resistance. Get a sheet of paper and brainstorm.

When you explore each of these, you can get closer to understanding what you are here to create. These may look simple. You could easily say that you love coaching, you are good at it, the world needs it, and you can get rewarded (paid) for it. No, no, no. Here you are going to dig deep and really think about this. For each of these, consider any challenges, lessons and gifts.

The Four Roles

Next, look at where the four questions intersect.

Passion – good and love

Mission – love and world needs

Profession – good and paid

Vocation – what the world needs, and you can get paid for

Passion – Good And Love

What are you passionate about?

Did you explore your passions? You may not be clear on what that is yet. As we said, you may be passionate about many things. We are looking for the one thing you could write about that resonates with you right now.

Mission – Love And World Needs

You hear of people with a mission who will do anything to support it. It's about the legacy they want to leave, what motivates them to get out of bed, and is very much values-based.

- How do you want to be remembered?
- What do you want to contribute to the world?
- What would you love to contribute to the world that would make you feel fulfilled?

My mission is...

Profession – Good And Paid

This is your job and usually something you are good at but may not love. Many people have no pre-defined career path; they just fall into something. Ask. Is that where you find yourself? How does it feel when you think about your profession? This is really asking you to examine what you are doing that pays the bills and ask how fulfilled you feel?

- What are you doing that pays the bills?
- What parts of your business (or job) do you enjoy?
- Where do you feel dissatisfied? Why?

Vocation – What The World Needs, And You Can Get Paid For

Vocation is what I used to think about nursing or caring. It's a real calling on your heart. You may get paid, but money is never what motivates you.

- What are the things that you do because they drive you in some way?

- Who will you support, no matter what?

Common Threads

When you look at passion, mission, profession and vocation, can you see any common threads or aspects? Think about this and ask what this tells you? Is there something that speaks to you now that informs the shape your book will take?

Satisfaction And Fulfilment

After exploring all of those aspects, we want to explore how much satisfaction and fulfilment you feel with what you are doing and writing this book? Pause and reflect. Then recheck in and ask where you feel the most fulfilment. Remember it is doing what you love, are good at, the world needs, and being paid for that which gives you fulfilment. Gets you thinking, doesn't it?

The Bottom Line

We want to get as close to doing what you love, that you are good at, the world needs, and you can get paid for, which is also meaningful and provides fulfilment. So it's important that your business is aligned with your values. Remember, we are all a work in progress, things will change, and you will change. But, most importantly, you need to write the right book, not just any old book.

Opportunities

The way to success is to become the first (or to be amongst the leaders) to do something. What can you see that other people don't? What opportunities are there right now that you can see that have been overlooked or not successfully exploited that you could turn into an excellent book?

The key is to **connect your passions (values, purpose and vision) to the available opportunities** and follow them through. Then, focus on one opportunity – the thing that will help you make your mark right now.

It's the jumble in your mind that restricts you; look at your passions. If you have eight things that rock your world, which path will lead you, right now, to the best opportunity. It is just about priorities. Your writing will flow, and you feel energy and enthusiasm when you are passionate about your book.

Remember to be curious, do not discount anything; what you may first think of as the best opportunity may become one for the future.

What are the current opportunities for you to exploit your passions? Take some time to reflect on what opportunities might exist for each thing you are passionate about. Then, after a period of reflection, decide *which* passion and opportunity for right now. You are looking for the one important opportunity which is a priority. This may change later, and that is ok. You may find that your opportunities become clearer when you go through your business strategy. In workshops, clients are often surprised by what leaps out at them.

For example, one client didn't realise that her passion for dogs would lead her to write about dogs and what they can teach you in business. It became clear that she could combine both things and use the book to promote her work and give to her favourite charity.

Now put your opportunities into priority order

Craft Your Brilliant Manifesto Before You Plan Your Book

A manifesto is a written statement which publicly declares your intentions, motives, or beliefs. It comes from the Latin manifestus - to manifest, to clearly reveal, to make real. Having a manifesto crystallises what you believe in and stand for. It is from here that you can create a statement about your book and personal brand.

I see it as the foundation from which you can build a platform, tribe or movement. You can connect the pieces of who you are, how you are being, what you do, why you do what you do, what you have to say and how you do it - values, passion, vision, purpose and inspirational message.

As the word suggests, you are using your manifesto to cement your vision, purpose, and inspirational message and bring about a manifestation of what you want to see and be in the world.

Are you ready to make a statement to the world?

How To Write A Brilliant Manifesto

Find the right place and time to write. Let the day go, put pen to paper, and trust what appears are the right words. Listen deeply. After a meditation or bath, take the next moments to hear what your heart and soul are saying. When you don't know what to write, ask for guidance and call in your muses. Then, when it comes, write it. It will make sense later. Are you ready?

Destroy The Elevator Pitch

Before you do anything, I want you to go and get the elevator pitch you have worked so hard on. This is the 30 to 60-second pitch you make at network meetings, which tells people your USP (unique selling proposition). Print, write it out and then burn it. Let go of the past perceptions of what you tell others.

The USP was invented back in the 1940s by an advertising agency. The idea was that you would promote one unique thing that no one else could deliver. The idea is that you can say buy me, for this one very different reason. That very different reason cannot be copied by your competitors and must have a strong pull so that you can pull in the consumers.

Think FedEx - When your package absolutely, positively has to get there overnight. What about Dominos Pizza? You get fresh, hot pizza delivered to your door in 30 minutes or less—or it's free, and my all-time favourite is Avis. We are number two, so we try harder.

Wouldn't it be more interesting if you could talk about the

experience your customer got from working with you and the results?

Review Values, Passion, IKIGAI, Vision, Purpose

- What are your distinct capabilities (knowledge, skills, experience, strengths, etc.?)
- What are your values?
- What values are most important to you?
- What do you want to be remembered for?
- What do you want to achieve?
- What are you passionate about?
- What is your IKIGAI?
- What is your vision?
- How will the message of your book manifest itself?
- How will you achieve your vision?
- What motivates you to achieve your vision?
- What is your purpose, your message and BIG WHY?
- Who is your message for?
- What value do they get from working with you?
- What are the top 5 experiences they feel when working with you?
- What do you believe about yourself and your message? (Or what you don't believe?)
- Write down - Here's what I know about myself and my message so far...
- What is sustainable about what you do or how you are

being?
- What is difficult to replicate?

Reflect

After you have read through the questions for exploration above, simply reflect. The reflection process is ongoing; things will keep coming to you. Notice what you notice and capture your insights.

Write – My Perfect Day

Go back to your last, my perfect day story. What do you see, hear, feel, smell, taste and know? You may have already done this. Do it again. To remind you, writing I will, or I am going to, is all future based. Writing instead, I am XYZ makes it more real, and thoughts become a reality.

Make A List Of 'Things'

As you read through your story, 'things' will pop out like the house you live in and the country you have moved to. It might include a fancy car or your jet. Equally, there may be aspects of your work, your purpose, where you are attracting and inspiring a certain type of person, something about your products and services and the amount of money you make. There may be things about your spirituality, nutrition, and other lifestyle factors. The idea is that you do not censor what you have written. You simply reduce it to a list. Use post-it notes. It's easier to move them around.

Sort The List - Subheadings

Now sort the list into an initial meaningful order, and create the subheadings for your manifesto. Leave and reflect.

Create Your Manifesto

The art now is to take your subheadings and list of things and re-order them so that they make sense to you. Then, under each, write a few words about what that 'thing' means. Reflect and re-write until it becomes something on which you can hang all your communications. Remember that your manifesto is not only about your message and book but also about the life you want to manifest from having written this book.

Reduce To A Short Statement

Create just one paragraph about your big why, book and personal brand.

Reduce To A Strapline

Find a few words that might be your 'strapline' or the title of your manifesto. These might be inspiring others to...

Create Your Experience Proposition

Who do you want to attract? What five experiences did you want someone to get when reading your book and working with you? What are the results of that experience?

For example

I work with conscious entrepreneurs who have an inspirational message that needs to be shared with the world. They want to discover who they are and find their voice. They want to create a business they love, rock their brand, write a book and turn their books into other products and services.

I make it simple to find out what you want to say and then create a stress-free approach to enabling you to share your message in a way that resonates with you. We'll do things like a review where you are and where you want to be. Create a strategy that maps to the outcomes you want. Find people, strategies and resources that work for you.

Actions and Checklist

Do the perfect day exercise to help you envision what you want

Write down your values and why they are important to you – what does this tell you?

Work on your passion and consider what your one passion for this book is

Do the Ikigai exercise. What do you learn? Are you still on the right track?

What is the greatest opportunity for you and your book right now?

Create a personal vision and a vision for your book

Create your purpose statement. How does this fit with the vision for your book and future?

Ask again – why you, and why your book?

Create your brilliant manifesto

Understanding Your Competitors

In this chapter, you will look at the competition to understand where your book will fit in and what gaps in the market you will fill.

A competitor analysis is done to better understand the market, the position you occupy and understand how to fill the gaps. A competitor analysis is great for crystallising where your book fits in with what is already available. It also informs your book strategy, tells you who your potential reader might be, what else they are buying, what their needs are, and gives you an idea about what kind of books and content is out there. You will see books you never knew existed, books you wished you had written, and a space for your work.

Why You Should Care About What Is Selling?

The authors who do best indeed are those who already have an audience hungry for what they are writing about. This may not be you (yet). And that's OK. If you don't have a huge platform of potential readers ready for your book, consider how you can build your platform now.

It's worth spending some time being strategic and thinking about how your book will sell and how to tweak your idea, so it's a better fit for the market. This doesn't mean you have to detract from the essence; it's being smart about leveraging what you know.

You should care about what else is selling because:

- It's easier to write when you know what to write and who you are writing for. The more specific and the clearer you

can be at the outset, the easier the writing
- It's going to be easier to sell your book because your reader is already looking for it
- It's easier to promote and market because there will be a built-in audience who wants to know what you are teaching or the story you are telling. It will be easier to get PR and publicity, promote to partners, get endorsements and reviewers, etc.
- You can match up what your reader wants to read with what you are an expert in (or have experience with) and what you want to achieve with your book

When it comes to writing, I like to see my fellow authors as collaborators instead of competitors; there is a place for all of us, as we each bring something different to our readers. Remember, just because there is a book with *that* title, the one you wanted to use, which looks like it covers your subject, it may not do it in the way that yours will, with your unique spin.

Find Out What Is Selling

So, let's do some homework and research your market and competitors. But, before you do, take some time for some keyword research.

Keyword Research

Keywords are the words and phrases that best describe your book's content and are the terms that searchers type into the text box in a search engine to discover books such as yours. Keyword research tells you what people are interested in and what they are looking for. Best of all, this provides great insights into creating your title and blurb because it tells you what kind of language your readers apply when searching for content. One of the best places to undertake your research is with Publisher Rocket.

If you were writing a book on dieting, you would expect to use words like diet, dieting, GI index, lose weight, etc. Make a list of all the keywords you might use to search for a book like yours.

- What keywords come up?
- How many searches are there for each per month?
- Are they relevant or not?
- What clues do you get for titles?

Once you have your keywords, head to an online book store and start researching titles, authors and books. Try randomly typing vaguely associated search terms and see what comes up.

Online Research

Go over to an online book store. Type your book topic into the search box. See what results come back. You can narrow it further if you want to. The store will give you suggestions.

Once you've found a good category. Play around and see what comes up. Have a browse around at those books. Find the ones that are selling the most.

Have a look at their table of contents. What topics do they cover?

How long are they? (eBook readers only gives you a rough page length and doesn't equate to a real page length. Don't worry too much about that.)

What else?

- What gaps can you see?
- Do you like them / don't like them?
- Under the book details, you can find:
- What other items do customers buy after viewing this item?
- Sponsored products related to this item
- Customers who bought this item also bought
- Explore these.
- What reviews are they getting – do the readers like them?
- What can you learn from the reviews?

Next, I want you to find **the online sellers bestseller rank** for a few books in your category. You'll find that in the product description. Get an idea of what kind of bestseller-ranking books in your category are reaching. Look at the author's profile – what does that tell you? Later you will want to create your author profile, so make a note to come back and do it. Finally, have a look at the description. Does it entice you to read the book? Did it match the table of contents, reviews and your expectations of what it was about? What did you learn? Copy the book cover graphic into a WORD document, later print this out and just observe what ideas come to your mind as you scan your competitors' work.

Competitors' Matrix

Thinking about your 'competitors', do the following:

- Make a list of the title, author, date of publication, price and best-seller ranking
- Explain why yours is different from each
- What is missing from their offerings?
- What segment of the marketplace is being neglected?
- What are they doing that seems to be working well?
- What do you think of their cover, the blurb and interior layout?

Read Your Competitors' Work

Once you have your competitors' matrix, choose a selection of books (no more than three) that resonate with you and buy them. Look on your bookcase; you may already own them. Read and learn. We can learn so much from what others do and say. Some of my clients make a point of not reading their competitor's work so that it doesn't distract them.

By looking at other writers and their books, you will get a good idea of how your voice will fit in and what sets you apart. The whole point of your competitive analysis is to help you see, get a feel for, and understand what's happening in your niche or genre and then determine how best to position yourself and your book. If you know what's happening, you will know how to differentiate yourself.

Modelling Others Books

There are a multitude of books that you could model yours on if you are stuck for ideas. Look at "50 shades of Grey"; how many people came up with ideas around the concept of 50 shades? What about Jack Canfield and his "Chicken Soup" series? Robin Sharma's "The Monk" series are great examples of books written to a formula that works very well for him.

Step 1

Make a list of evaluation criteria. You will use these to assess your competitors' work as you read and review their books. E.g.

- Writing is easy to understand
- Uses lists
- Has diagrams and drawings
- Has action plans
- Uses simple words
- Pages are laid out so that the book is easy to read and digest
- Understands their reader
- Arguments are well explained
- Research is clearly defined
- They use an easy-to-read framework
- They make their key principles easy to understand

Step 2

Evaluate each of the criteria for the three books you are reviewing.

- What do you like about the books?
- What don't you like?
- What does that tell you?
- How will you use that information?

Step 3

Write a review of one (or all) of the books

- What makes your book different?
- What key points have been left out?
- Which readers are not being addressed?

What Else Can You Find Out About Your Competitors?

After browsing around your online publisher, surf the internet and look at your competitors' websites and social media, what can you learn from them? Then, armed with this research, ask how does your book fill a gap? What else can you learn about how they market themselves? What tips can you pick up? Who do they collaborate with? What about their personal branding? What can you do better?

And don't forget to ask others, friends and family about the books they have bought in the genre you hope to serve.

Actions and Checklist

Complete a 'competitors' matrix.'

Ask – do you know why these books are selling well?

Ask – what did you learn from your competitors' research?

Scan-read one book and ask what can you learn about how it has been constructed?

Who Do You Want To Inspire?

In this chapter, you will explore who you want to inspire with your book and your message. Think about how well you know the ideal reader for your book. People buy books because of the outcome, solution or result it gives them.

When I first started to write, I wrote for myself. There were things that needed clarity in both my life and my business. Way back when I was consulting in marketing, I had books on how to conduct a marketing audit and how to write a marketing plan. I wrote them because I wanted to show my clients how easy it was to go through a process, answer some questions, and provide direction and an outcome.

At that time, I didn't sit down and decide who might be my ideal reader. I simply consolidated what I did and knew to be a process that worked. Just as when I was in the training business and wrote manuals, I didn't have a map of who I was writing for. What I knew was I had to make the process of using software (at that time) easy.

When I started to support people with journaling and healing through writing, the notion of an ideal customer started to make more sense. I can remember drawing endless pictures of who these people were and what writing a book as a healing tool would give them.

I wouldn't write a book these days without my scruffy diagrams and ideal reader archetypes. Certainly, when I sat down to write edition 2 of Writing To Heal, I knew that my ideal reader was someone who loves to write and journal and understands the healing power of writing. These people have been through trauma and need to make sense of their life.

I wrote the book's first edition because I needed to create clarity around the processes I taught and coached. I wanted to inspire my reader to go deeper into the healing process for the second edition.

For this book, my ideal reader is someone who wants to write a book to build their brand. They want a clear process that will enable them to get their ideas out, know which is the right idea, and get their book properly planned and written. They like to plan (their way...), and they like steps that make things simple.

Who Is Your Ideal Reader?

How well do you know the wants and needs of your ideal reader? When you write, you are looking to connect to one reader. A single reader. Why?

- Much easier to write because we are speaking to that person
- It will make a better book, one which creates a connection
- When you understand them, you can ensure that you write to emotionally engage them
- It is more likely to be read and enjoyed. If we write for one reader, they will (more likely) implement what we are teaching, will enjoy what we have to say
- When you adjust your voice to your reader, it becomes just as if you were talking face to face
- It is more likely to sell. There is a place for a book as a personal journey for ourselves, but the reality is that most of us want our books to sell and to be read

It may not seem like a 'nice' idea to see your reader as a self-centred creature only out for what they can get, but the reality is that our reader wants to know WIIFM - what's in it for me? Unless it is a present for someone else, they will not buy your book on *"better health for menopausal women"* if they are a young gad-about-town twenty-something. Menopause is far away and is what their granny has, isn't it?

For clarity, a target market is made up of buyers and readers:

Buyers – people we attract to buy (these will be the reader and anyone who buys for others)

Readers – these are the ones we want to connect to and communicate with emotionally

Readers and buyers = your audience

Knowing who your buyers and readers are and why you are writing for them will help you clarify what to write about

Keep asking yourself:

- Who are you writing for? Who do you want to inspire? This might be you, someone like you, someone you have solved a problem for, the you that you used to be or another reason
- If you were buying this book, why?
- Who do you think your ideal reader is right now?

Knowing who your ideal reader is makes it easier to write for them because *we can speak directly to them*. By speaking directly to them, we have a better chance of making a connection. By connecting, we have a better opportunity to sell more books or supplemental products and services.

Pin-Pointing Your Reader

To help you get closer to your ideal reader, you can utilise market classifications tools, which help you segment the market that your reader may sit in. It may not be something that an author usually thinks about when determining what their book may be about. However, it will provide invaluable insight into how to address your reader's needs. Naturally, I understand this is not something many mentors cover, but have a go and see what you discover.

Traditional Market Segmentation

Segmentation aims to identify unique markets with similar attributes and find profitable segments. Common market segment dimensions:

- **Demographic and Geographic location** – These affect the size of the market and the reader's needs, desires, and usage
- **Demographic** – E.g. age, sex, income, education, household size, homeownership, etc.
- **Geographic** – Where they are located, both physical and virtual

- **Behavioural needs, attitudes, and buying patterns** – These affect the product and promotion variables, as well as the how your topic enables them to meet their needs
- **Behavioural** – The processes your reader uses to select, buy and use your books. Or how they think, feel, reason, and choose between different books and authors
- **Psychological** – Urgency of needs satisfaction. People often purchase books when they discover something that needs dealing with now. You are also looking for psychological attitudes such as aspirations, interests, opinions, lifestyle, etc.

Get Into The Detail

(Kottler 1984) suggested that for market segmentation to be effective, all segments must be:

Distinct – each segment is different from other segments. This means that different marketing mixes will be necessary

Accessible – how your readers and buyers can be reached?

Measurable – how easily can we measure the segment?

Profitable – is the segment large enough to provide a stream of constant future revenue and profit? For example, will lots of people buy your books?

It's important that you get as clear a picture as possible to tailor your writing and marketing activities to each segment. Also, consider the other products and services you will create from this book when doing this exercise and who you want to target with them.

Reader Archetypes

Coming up with 'your reader archetype' is a lot of fun. This is where you create a written profile of your reader, looking at what they may read or watch, what they drink, and where they go on holiday. Who are their friends? And what type of people would they cross the street to avoid?. Are they married or single? Do they have pets, and what kind? What's keeping them awake at night (and how can you make it go away)? Think about the symptom and the root of the problem – and what their life will look like when the problem is solved. What do they want that they don't need? What do they need that they don't want? Finally (a really important one...), what would they hate to miss out on?

Give them a name and life. When you have finished, leave it and reflect; then come back and draw your ideal reader. After this, collect pictures of things that connect you to your reader and create a reader mood board.

Are They Head, Heart Or Intuitive?

Heart

This reader works from their heart and wants a book that will connect with their passion and purpose and guide them to make their world a better place. They will have a journal by the side of their bed and will write about how they can turn what they learn into something useful for the world.

Head

This reader is practical, and they like systems and processes. You will find them setting goals and using your book to create accountability. Your book will teach them something practical.

Intuitive

This reader wants a book which asks them to dive deeply into their feelings. They want to be guided on how to explore what your message means to them. They want to evolve and support others to evolve, expand and transform.

Are They One Or All?

Your reader can be one or all the above. When you structure your book, consider who you want to speak to. When designing a chapter framework, decide which part speaks to which reader.

Have some fun with this. Never get caught up trying to analyse it to the nth degree. It may also evolve as you write. What if you discover that your reader is not who you were expecting?

There are many ways to classify your reader; have a go and come back after a period of reflection. You should be able to get clearer.

Knowing your ideal reader is one part of knowing what the heart spot for your book

Now Go A Little Deeper

Go back to your online publisher and look at the "also bought" lists. What does this tell you about your reader? Are they into personal development, or do they have an interest in psychology?

What are your potential readers saying in the reviews? You may have already done this, in which case, remind yourself:

What keywords did you use to find books in your genre?

Which blogs does your ideal reader read and comment on?

Which groups do your readers lurk and play in?

Read their Twitter streams. Who do they interact with, and what do they Tweet?

Where else are they hanging about? Instagram or maybe Pinterest?

What Questions Does Your Book Answer?

The next piece of the jigsaw is the questions your book answers or the problems it solves. Think outside of who you currently consider your ideal reader to be. Who asks you what questions? Who are they, and what will they get from reading your book?

30 Questions

Choose 30 questions that your book answers for your ideal reader. If you know these, it is easier to stay on track when you come to writing your content and connecting with your reader. E.g. How do I create an outline for my book?

These questions can be used for chapter headings and then classified under chapter headings as the questions each chapter answers.

Problem And Results

You have 30 questions. Next, look at them through the eyes of the potential problems your readers may have. Then, looking at your questions, consider all the potential problems and write these down per question. Next, consider your solution and the results your reader will get. Finally, write what you believe the benefits will be for your readers—for example, a book on nutrition and sleep.

- **Problem**: My sleep is disturbed
- **Results**: By understanding which foods help you to produce the right chemicals in your brain, you can change your diet and learn to sleep well
- **Benefits**: You will sleep better and be able to enjoy life

Look at each of the problems and ask yourself if this were my problem:

- How do I feel?

- Why do I feel this way?
- What are the facts?
- What do I know to be true?
- What don't I know?
- What do I have?
- What don't I have?
- What other forces are influencing this problem?
- What if I could solve it?
- How might I solve it?

Do this for as many problems you think your book will help your reader solve. Then, once you have worked out each of the problems and how they will be resolved, you can map them into chapters.

If You Were Your Reader

Close the ideal reader puzzle and ask, what would I be reading if I were my reader? Is there a pattern to your buying habits? What seduces you into buying six books on the same subject? Look at your bookshelf. What leaps out at you? Which are your top ten favourite books, and why?

The Hook

Your book must be enjoyable, engaging, easy to read and motivating. You want your reader to take action or get a result/outcome from reading your book. Thinking about what will hook your reader helps clarify and cement what your book is about and how it will draw in your potential reader. Things to entice them include the title and subtitle, the blurb, how you create emotional connections, good chapter introductions, your content that leaves your reader asking questions of themselves, and your writing that keeps their attention. And remember, it is all about them and not what you think.

Actions and Checklist

Do all of the 'who is my reader' exercises and design your ideal reader profile

Put your reader profile on the wall and keep refining it. Keep looking at it as you work your way through the rest of this book and your plan

The Book Blurb And Titles

Now that you have worked out who your reader is, this chapter will help you write your book blurb/pitch and title so that you can connect with them emotionally and invite them to explore more about your book.

Book Blurb / Pitch (Description)

The blurb is the written sales pitch on the back of your book. It provides your potential reader with an insight into your book. The book blurb should arouse curiosity rather than provide concrete answers. We are looking at how you can draw your reader to "Look Inside", browse through the first pages and make a purchase. The blurb is the invitation to read more and entice your reader to purchase your book.

How To Craft A Blurb

Read the blurbs of books you own; what attracted you to them?

What do you like or dislike about the way the blurb is presented?

Take the ones you like. What do they all have in common?

Take three books whose blurb hooks you in and model yours on theirs

Imagine if you had 15 seconds to sell your book. What would be in those vital seconds?

What are the benefits? In this book, you will learn…

How will your book fulfil its promise?

Is this the first of its kind?

Practice Writing Your Blurb

Write three versions of your blurb. Try them from different perspectives or starting points. Then, read each of them aloud; what needs to change? Have you repeated any words? Have you covered the senses of seeing, feeling and hearing (if relevant)?

See: We will show you how to….

Feel: We will touch on….

Hear: If you like the sound of x, then you will….

These may not all be relevant. Most blurbs use visual words – "we will show you."

Leave them for a few days for reflection

Use Another Book As A Template

In my courses, I reference a book by Nancy Kline called a Time to Think. Her blurb is inspiring and uses powerful words.

Over the past 15 years, Nancy Kline has identified 10 behaviours that form a system called a Thinking Environment, a model of human interaction that dramatically improves the way people think and thus the way they work and live. The power of effective listening is recognised as the essential tool of good management.

In this book, Kline describes how we can achieve this and presents a step-by-step guide that can be used in any situation.

Whether you want to have more productive meetings, solve business problems or build stronger relationships, this book offers you a new world of possibilities.

Use Powerful Words

Over the past 15 years

Nancy Kline has identified 10 behaviours

That form a system

That dramatically improves the way people think, and thus the way they work and live

The power of

Presents a step-by-step guide

That can be used in any situation

More productive meetings, solve business problems or build stronger relationships

This book offers you a new world of possibilities

Try and follow this template and then rewrite it as your own.

Letter To

Imagine writing a letter to your friend who knows you and your subject matter well; describe your book. Now do the same thing for someone you don't know. What considerations did you have to make for the person that you know and for the stranger? Now rewrite your blurb.

What Title And Why?

This is often the hardest part of the book process. How can you create a title that will hook your ideal reader as they are browsing the many books in your category? Let's explore.

What Are The Goals Of Your Book?

What is your book about? What are its goals, and what do you want your reader to do as a result of reading it? Start with your goals.

- Do you want to build a brand and become known for what?
- Perhaps you want to launch a program or online course
- Maybe it's about kick-starting or building on your speaking career

Brainstorm until you get something that resonates with you and the ideas, concepts and outcome you want your reader to get. Do not dismiss anything. Do this first, as this will help you find the right title and subtitle.

Consider what ideas, concepts and outcomes you want your book title to convey. This will help you find the right title and subtitle. Then create a swipe file of book covers with titles you like and don't like, and work out why.

A good title won't help you sell your book, but it will give it a fighting chance. On the other hand, an obscure title will not help at all unless you are very well-known.

The Buying Process

Buyers go through a process when they buy a book. First, think about how you buy a book. Is it the title, the blurb, the cover, or is it something else? They may be looking for something specific, so they browse that category. They may have asked for a recommendation which leads them to that category. They look at:

- Titles and subtitles
- Cover
- The back blurb - the book's description
- They look inside at the chapter titles
- The author bio and may go off to research them more
- The price
- You want to:
- Keep it simple
- Grab attention
- Encourage action

The title, including the subtitle, must give the reader an idea of what the book is about.

What Kind Of Title?

Catchy? Doesn't say much but acts as a disruptor. The subtitle says it all. OR. Does what it says on the tin – highly descriptive. Whichever you go for, consider how your subtitle will cement that.

Subtitles

Describe the outcome or what the reader will get.

7 steps to

The formula to

Secrets that will

How to

How to x in y easy steps

How to x the right way

If you are writing a series of books, consider how you can become known for the person that... For example, do you offer formulas for something? Each book you write will have the formula for whatever it is as a subtitle.

Try A Headline Creator Tool

At the time of writing, I use a fabulous tool from Co-schedule (https://coschedule.com/headline-analyzer), which helps me to craft titles for my blogs. You can use this for your subtitles. Imagine that you are writing a book on the dieting industry. Your working title might be:

Six weeks to a new you – What the dieting industry does not tell you. (Sub-title)

Chapter one of your book on dieting could be a review of the dieting industry and might be called: The dieting industry, a review

Or it could be called:

My affair with the diet, learn how my mistakes could save your life

The second title has much more impact and promises what's to come. Again, the key is getting something written and remembering – perfection kills creativity.

The CONE Method For Creating Titles

After playing with lots of ideas, I like to do the CONE test and ask myself these reflective questions.

Curiosity – how will you pique their curiosity even if they were not looking for a book like this?

Outcome – this is your promise. What do they get from reading the book?

Needs – does it address a need in your ideal reader?

Emotion – using power words to create an emotional connection. What emotional needs do you want to connect with?

Final Thoughts

- Brainstorm your ideas
- Start with long titles and then make them shorter and shorter until they are one word
- Narrow down your ideas
- Think keywords and what someone might search for on Google or your online publisher
- What are the benefits or the outcome?
- Remember your ideal reader
- What problems does your book solve?
- Could there be a number of steps or laws?
- Consider metaphors, alliterations, slang and popular phrases
- Could you coin a new phrase?
- Ask if someone asked me what the title of my book was, would I have to go into a lengthy explanation of what it is about, or does it make sense with the title and subtitle?
- Don't overthink
- Make it easy to say
- Visualise and imagine others talking about your book. How does it feel to have your title mentioned? What do you think the reaction of the others in the conversation might be?
- Pick your favourites and test them
- Make a mock cover and place it with your book vision board

Actions and Checklist

Write your blurb and play with it until it feels right, for right now. Then, you can refine it when you come to the cover design stage.

Write down some titles and subtitles that you think would resonate

Add your blurb and titles to your reader picture

Your Book And Business Strategy

In this chapter, you will consider what you will be using your book for – your book business strategy.

Your Book, Brand And Business Must Be Aligned

Books often fail to get written because your brand and business are not aligned with your book. Every business has a core message, and the book must echo that.

Business is about where you are, where you want to go, and how you will get there. A brand is who you are, what you want to be known for, and how you will communicate it. Your book (content and message) is a vehicle for your message. It forms part of your delivery system.

Are You Doing What You Really Want To?

Consider your business. Are you doing what you love, are good at, which the world needs, and you will get paid for? Review your IKIGAI. Many people start to write a book only to find that it drags up 'stuff' that needs to be dealt with. This happens to successful people too. Suddenly they see in putting pen to paper, they have a different yearning. This needs to be addressed first.

Core Message

Your core message is part of your focus and how you inspire others. It's what you are here to do. It's based on the theme or themes we uncovered, and it will be based on your IKIGAI.

Every product and service, including and especially including your books and courses, need a core message. People connect to us emotionally, and because of this, we need to tell stories in a way that touches an emotional need.

Your core message answers questions. People are always looking for solutions to something, and by answering that need, you are delivering value and a feeling of value. Others will feel inspired and motivated by how they perceive you have supported them. And we all know that word-of-mouth referral is very powerful. In summary:

- Every person/business has a core message
- It is your identity and the identity of your brand
- Your message, your business, your book and you are connected
- It is based on a theme(s), your calling, your IKIGAI
- Each product and service ties into this
- Your message needs to create images, tell stories, and move people emotionally
- It needs to answer questions, solve problems and deliver value
- Inspires and motivates them to buy your products and services because of the value you add to their lives

What Is Your Core Message?

The core message of your business and book need to complement each other. The core message is your and your book's identity. But it goes deeper than that. Knowing what this is means that you can market yourself and your books and other assets easier. Your voice and message need to be consistent throughout everything. Points to consider.

- Identify the need or challenge you address
- What is your solution or approach? What is unique or different about what you do?
- Describe the positive results. Challenge, solution, and results all wrapped in a good story

E.g. If you are a self-love coach, your core message could be about teaching others to learn how to love themselves. Because it creates a strong foundation for their life and helps your reader/customer find inner peace and contentment.

- What is your business's core message?
- What is the core message of your book?
- How do the two connect?

Write a core message statement. Leave it and reflect. You can always come back and refine it.

Create A Clear Strategy

It takes approximately seven seconds to form an impression – some say less. Your book gives you instant credibility. A beautifully crafted book will help you stand out, captivate your readers, and put you miles ahead of your competitors; it opens up new opportunities for alliances, speaking gigs, and creating new products and services. So, before you rush off to pen your bestselling brand-building business book, let's take a reality check.

A book is part of your overall business strategy; it is not *the* strategy. When working with my clients, the conversation is about their business vision and considering how their book will help bring that alive.

Sometimes the conversation is about how do I get out of corporate life and create my entrepreneurial business? This is when getting a salary while writing your book is a blessing.

Remember, it is a rare author who makes a mint from books alone. The key is to see your book as a product and not a creative outlet. You need to use your entrepreneurial mindset to visualise it as a product you have designed to open up other opportunities. If one of your business objectives is to become an after-dinner speaker, your book could lead the way to your first engagement. That speaking opportunity will recoup the cost of writing your book.

Even bestselling "Chicken Soup for the Soul" is much more than 'just' books. The creators turned their speaking careers into books and then built a personal development community. They have sold millions of copies and now also sell greetings cards, flowers and even pet food.

The great news is that having a book to help you to elevate your business is even more accessible than ever. This is because it is easier than ever, with companies offering publishing through their publishing platforms to publish your brand-building book.

Book sales are just one small piece of your marketing armoury. If you spend your energy marketing your higher-priced products and services based on your book, you will bring in more income and build greater influence. It is worth remembering that the sales of products and services, including speaking and workshops, will impact your bottom line more than what you make from direct sales of books (unless you are very lucky).

Many entrepreneurial authors don't look to book sales as a source of income, preferring to give away copies of their books. Instead, they use books as marketing tools (lead magnets) to bring other benefits and income. They invest in producing the best possible book to exploit that book to create business opportunities that will bring in real income.

Questions To Ask Yourself

Do you need to be seen as an authority in your field? Having a book will help you to be able to reach a larger audience

Do you want to reach more people with your message? Books are distributed globally, and your message can be read worldwide. And from there, you can consider how you can maximise that opportunity

Do you need to develop your brand? Having a book will raise your profile and help to establish you as a credible go-to source for your subject matter

What else can you create from your book? Webinars, online courses, retreats and workshops are just some of the things that you can develop from your book

Consider Different Ways To Get Your Message Out There As You Write A Book

There are many ways to write a book. When I talk about writing a book, I refer to content that could become a book. Your strategy may be to start with an e-book of between 5000 and 12000 words which you use as a lead magnet. This could go onto a blog you have planned as a book, and in this instance, you are blogging your book. I realise that you write blogs differently from books, but with some imagination and editing of your base content, you will have a great head start.

There are many benefits to doing this. You can build your list and brand and test your content on your ideal customer first.

What Or Where Are Your Greatest Opportunities?

Is there one opportunity that currently speaks to you? Consider which book idea that might be. When you know which opportunity, consider how you will exploit it. What are the steps to bringing that idea to market? Then consider your product development roadmap. You are looking for the most relevant opportunities to exploit now.

Knowing your business strategy is one part of the puzzle. Review who the reader of this book is and how you can address their needs, concerns or challenges. If you have several ideas, consider a series of books. Remember to exploit each book before you bring your next book to market.

Actions and Checklist

Define the core message of your business, brand and book

Create an outline business strategy (one part of the heart spot)

Let's Get Brainstorming

This chapter is about brainstorming before you sit down to decide the heart spot and create your full outline and chapter framework. It's worth doing to just get it all out.

Choose A Brilliant Book Topic And Get Clear On Your Book's Big Message

Whether you have a million book ideas or can't drum up a single one, it's important to start by getting clear on your book. You want to think about why this book will do for you and your brand and what you want to create in the world with it.

Get clear. Otherwise, confused readers will likely put the book down and wonder if you're truly the expert you claim to be.

When you have very little time to write your book, it's best to choose a topic that you're:

- Familiar with
- Passionate about
- Confident will sell

Familiarity will help the writing flow so you can accomplish more in the little time you have. Passion will fuel your desire to sit down and write. Finally, confidence will motivate you to get out and market your book when it's complete.

Other questions (many of which you will have already explored) to ask yourself before settling on a book topic are:

- What's my #1 area of expertise?
- What do I want to be known for?

- What is the biggest struggle of my ideal clients or customers?
- What story or message do I want to shout from the rooftops?
- Will I be okay speaking on this subject for months or years to come? (Your book topic often positions your speaking platform)
- What do I feel is important to share with my audience?
- Will I be able to effectively bring this topic to life and provide readers with what they need? (Answer this one objectively and push any limiting beliefs to the side)
- What results or outcomes can readers expect to receive from the book?
- To get those results, what do readers need to know, understand, or do?

This last question can help you decide what information to actually include in your book to help them get their desired result. Your book may be the first introduction to new people in your audience, so you don't need to give away all your secrets inside. Instead, promise a result and deliver, but leave your readers wanting more from you (i.e., joining your coaching program or purchasing another product).

If these questions sound familiar, you're right. They are the same questions you'd ask before creating a product. Every product you sell – including this book – is a reflection of you and your business, so it makes sense that you'd ask the same questions.

Also, consider what you're currently selling. Think about your (current) signature packages, courses and programs. Is there a way to somehow tie your programs into your book so your book becomes a marketing vehicle not just for you but for your specific programs? Maybe you can reference your program in the book by suggesting that working with you would be the best next step after reading the book.

The first exercise is all about brainstorming book topics. There are two different ways to approach this. One where you put your ideas in columns and one where you create a Venn diagram.

Create these in your journal. Write down topics you're familiar with in one column or circle, passionate about/want to write about in another circle, and what you're sure will sell in the third. The Venn Diagram will allow you to see where these three topics overlap. Then, pick a topic from that category that seems most interesting or exciting to you. And there you have it! Your book topic is decided.

The second exercise is about asking your audience to choose one of your three favourite topics. This fun engagement exercise helps move you out of analysis paralysis and into writing.

Our last exercise is writing a one-sentence statement that describes what your book is about, who it's for, and what they'll learn by the end. This may change as you get deeper into the writing, but it's important to do this now to start writing with a set theme for your book.

Brainstorm Book Topics

Create a chart in your journal with three sections and brainstorm these:

- Topics you're familiar with
- Topics you're passionate about
- Topics you're sure will sell

Then pop them in a Venn diagram like this, and hopefully, the one in the middle is THE book.

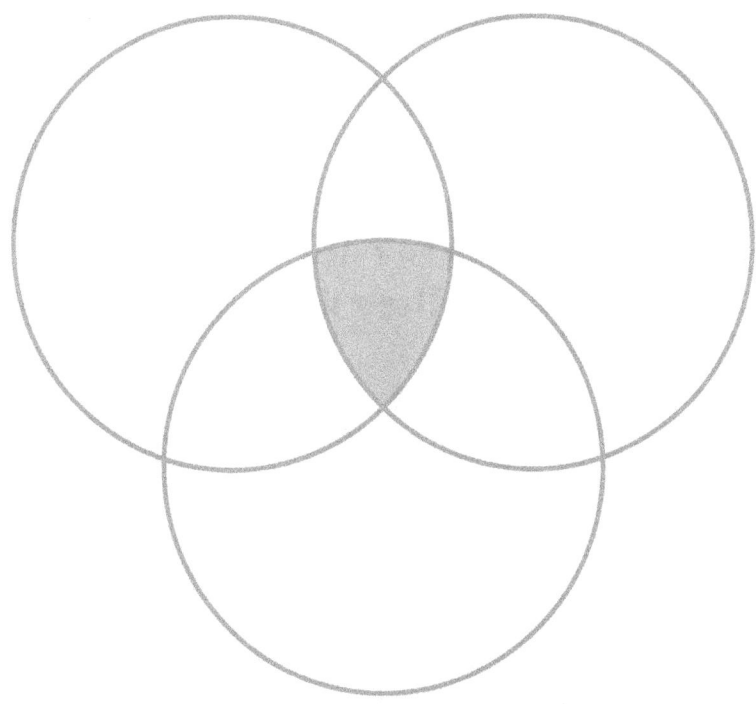

Struggling With The "Sure To Sell" Bit?

Use these questions to survey your coaching clients, customers, email subscribers and/or your social media following to help them choose your next topic. Chart the results.

Survey/Poll Questions (For Your Readers)

- What is your biggest struggle?
- Which of these topics resonates with you the most, and why?
- What topic or problem area would YOU like me to discuss in my next book, and why?
- What would make you want to read a book that covers the topic or problem area above?
- What outcome would you expect to get?

Write A One-Sentence Statement That Describes What Your Book Is About, Who It's For And What They'll Learn By The End Of It

Consider this your condensed elevator speech for your book. The more concise, the better it will be and easier to remember as you write and tell people about this new venture.

- My book is about...
- My book is for...
- My readers will learn...

Brain Dump Your Brilliance And Craft Compelling Chapter Ideas

Many entrepreneurs have ideas swirling in their brains day and night, thus making it slightly difficult to focus on just one topic or project at a time. If you have too many ideas in your own brain, employ the 'brain dump' method in your weekly routine. Sunday evenings are great for this.

Brain dumping simply means writing down all the ideas in your head. Scribble everything down and then separate your book ideas and work on these. This brain dump list is the basis for planning out what you actually want to say and include in your book.

Most importantly, keep your big book idea foremost in your mind when planning. Then, you will use the rest of your book to help your reader get from where they are to where you want them to be. Also, keep their pain points in mind because your book's promise should be to answer those questions and/or solve that problem. This might be taking them through an actual process, or it might be more about helping them experience a mindset shift around your topic of expertise.

For example, if you are a nutritionist who has healed Osteoporosis naturally and supports others to do this, then each chapter within the book will take the reader through part of the process. For example, chapter 1 might be titled – 10 things to think about before starting your healing project, chapter 5 might be – working with your doctor, and chapter 7 might be steps to discover your root cause. Then you would discuss all the natural ways to heal once you have sorted out the root cause.

All the important processes would have their own chapter titles.

Or you might craft your book around WHY natural healing is more effective than taking drugs (this, of course, could be very emotionally charged – but you are here to lead with your ideas). You're not walking them through a process but rather helping them see the benefits of natural healing or maybe busting popular myths about how to heal bones naturally. Instead of teaching them a process, you're enabling a shift in mindset.

There's no right or wrong way to do this. In fact, there are about a million ways to get the inspiration and structure you need for your book, and you should just choose whatever feels right to you.

You can also create a mind map, use an Excel spreadsheet, post-it notes, an art journal, or use a big old whiteboard to get your ideas out of your head. The best medium or format is the one you'll use consistently. I love a roll of brown wrapping paper and coloured pens.

Your first exercise in this step is a simple brain dump. Use this space to brainstorm ANYTHING and EVERYTHING you might want to include in your book. Don't edit yourself yet (that comes later). You'll also see some prompts that can help spur those creative juices.

The second exercise is about choosing your chapters. Your exact chapter titles don't have to be decided right now but mapping out what you want to talk about in which order is certainly helpful. There are no strict rules about how many chapters you can include in your book. I tend to aim for between 10 and 15 for non-fiction books, so you can use that as a rough number. These days people like shorter books. Most of my books come out at 40-50k words.

Write down the tentative title and/or big topic of each chapter. Ensure each chapter makes one main point and does not cover too much information. For example, I like to write out 3 questions this book answers to help me. Chapters are great because they divide your book into easily digestible chunks for people, so they get through your book and get the transformation step by step.

Brain Dump

Brainstorm the stories and research you'll need to create supporting evidence for each chapter. Since each chapter will have its own big idea, you'll then spend your chapter' backing up' that big idea with stories and research – either your own or others. The knowledge audit later builds on this. As you start fleshing this out, make sure to include information, stats, or stories from the following:

- Client case studies
- Personal stories from your own life (my favourite)
- Quotes from others
- Statistics and research papers from others (or yourself, of

course!)
- Other books
- Magazine or news articles on your topic(s) or related topic

Remember, these ideas are fluid, so they can be changed and adapted once you start writing.

Journal Prompts to Aide Brainstorming

Bring to mind your signature process. Each chapter of your book is focused on one part of the process

[#] questions people ask about your topic of expertise. Each question–and answer becomes its own chapter.

[#] steps to achieve [outcome]. What exact steps would you need to take someone through to get from where they are to where they want to be by the end of your book)?

[#] lessons on the road to [outcome]

[#] misconceptions about [your topic]–and the truth

[#] lessons you'd tell yourself if you were starting over in [your topic of expertise]

[#] taboo topics when it comes to [outcome]

[#] mistakes most people make when starting to [outcome/topic of expertise]

Choose Your Chapters

It's time to narrow down your ideas, so you know exactly what you will be writing about. Write down the tentative title and/or big topic of each chapter. We will visit chapter titles later.

Right now, open your journal and write without thinking too much ten chapter titles.

Craft A Short, Simple Outline For Book Writing With Ease

Writing is a unique process, and there's no 'right' or 'wrong' way to do it. However, most writers benefit from creating at least a loose outline before trying to write an entire book. Consider this a roadmap for your book. Mapping out an outline allows you to move chapters around, so they make more sense and prevent you from adding extraneous stories, stats, or information that doesn't directly relate to your main topic.

That said, an outline is fluid and can be adjusted, but seeing it in front of you will help you stay on track instead of veering off into tangents.

Traditional outlines include A table of contents, chapter titles or main points, and any number of bullet points under each chapter that support that chapter's main point.

What are these bullet points, exactly? Include any explanation, discussions, statistics, and information you need or want to include to explain the chapter. Include supporting stories and research plus bullet points for THESE points you're making.

If you ever find yourself getting off track or feeling like you're including too much or too little in a chapter, ask yourself what your reader absolutely must know by the end of each chapter in order to make progress. You should include those points and save the other stuff for another project.

When your outline is complete, review it and see if it flows from start to finish. Feel free to move things around, like switching chapters from one place to another or moving bullet points from one chapter to another where it makes more sense. The outline flow should feel easy and connected.

Remember this isn't set in stone, but rather to ensure you get it all down on paper and don't 'forget' anything when you get to writing. You can continue updating this outline as you write and think of any new ideas you might want to include.

This exercise is about organising your thoughts into an outline. Use your previous exercises' topic and chapter ideas and add bullet points.

Write A Simple Chapter Outline

Open a document and write your chapter titles, bullet points, and research from the previous exercises. Start here with a rough outline, and in the next chapter, you will look at chapter outlines in depth. Use this as inspiration and do it for each chapter:

Actions and Checklist

Do all of the exercises and get everything out of your head, ready to decide on the heart spot and create your full outline and framework

The Heart Spot

In this chapter, you will bring together your vision, the reader, content and business strategy with a review of everything you have done to cement your one book idea.

How Do I Find The Heart Spot For This Book?

Unless we are very clear about where we are going relative to the position on the map, your book may end up reaching for the moon, aiming for the stars, or worse still, wavering between all points on the compass.

The heart spot for your book is where your vision, the business strategy, the reader you are writing for, and the most relevant conte*nt* intersect. Unfortunately, as writers and subject matter experts, we tend to want to cram too much in.

Review Time

Review the previous chapters and have your plan to hand. Have you created a plan, and does it feel like it will work for you? Where are the gaps? Do you need to review anything before you move ahead?

Once you have mapped the four parts, where they intersect is your heart spot for THIS BOOK.

- **Vision**: Where do your personal, brand, business, and book vision intersect? Your vision will have an impact on how you write, present and market your book
- **Reader:** You now know who you are speaking to when you write your book. You know what problems you solve for them

- **Content:** You will now either have the ONE idea or have a few ideas for your book. What came out of the brainstorming? These ideas could be worth pursuing; however, we are looking for the **ONE idea – your ONE THING for right now**. When you have clarity, you can start to think about which content you will use, write or research to fill the gaps (see knowledge audit later to uncover this)
- **Strategy**: You will know how you will use your book, which will shape how you write and present your content. It will also inform you of what else needs to be done to go alongside the book to ensure that it is the right book for your business and brand

Decision time: What is the ONE book you will write NOW?

Heart, Gut, Head

There is one more test…Which book idea speaks to your heart, intuitively feels right, and your head tells you it makes the most sense to write? Work it through in that order: -

- Heart – this is where your true book lies
- Intuition – this is a check
- Head – this looks at commercial sense and reality

There may be many books which you could write. There will be one that is right for you, right now. After all of the discovery and mapping out of your ideas, you have to choose. Which ONE is it?

The Working Title

Finally, give your book a working title, if you haven't already done so, to bring your book alive. If you have a title, review it and make this the first thing you see when you open your binder.

Actions and Checklist

Decide on the heart spot for this book

Create your best working title and put it up where you can see it

Creating Outlines And Frameworks

Good books don't just happen; they are designed, or should I say, outlined. This chapter will help you create a clear structure, a pathway from one chapter to the next, and provides direction, connecting each chapter to the overall theme and answering questions that our readers may have. Most importantly, it makes your book easier and faster to write. There are several ways to get to the outline; my favourite is 'Step it out', followed by mind mapping and storyboarding. Have everything from the brainstorming in the previous chapter to hand.

Step It Out – The Book Flow

This is a walking, using your intuition and making sense process, which will help cement your chapter outlines and what you did in the brainstorming section.

Get some A4 sheets of paper (10 to 12 will be perfect) and a voice recorder (use the one on your phone). Then, if you have a friend or partner, use them to ask you questions about each chapter:

- What is this chapter about?
- What is this chapter's main point?
- What 3 questions does this chapter answer?
- What will my reader get from it?
- Why is it important for my reader to know this? Why is it essential I share this?
- How can they (your reader) do the same, or what exercises can I share? You could include questions, a case study or a personal story
- What if – what are the benefits of following the advice in this chapter, or the consequences of not? Invite the reader to imagine what-ifs?
- What are the chapter thinking points and call to action?

Ask your partner to write down any key points for you. The writing helps you and your partner to remember key points. Use the voice recorder; it is invaluable for remembering everything you say. You could additionally record this as a video as a backup. Find somewhere quiet to work and some floor space.

Discovering Your Book Outline

- Turn on your voice recorder, and make sure you have enough space to record
- Using one sheet of paper per chapter, start laying the A4 sheets out on the floor
- Either lay them in a straight line or in a circle
- As you step onto each sheet, pause to reflect, close your eyes and go inside to get a feeling, sense or image of what the chapter might be about
- Using the voice recorder, talk out loud and ask the questions listed
- As you step onto the next chapter, consider if and how they logically flow into each other. Can you feel the connection? Make a note of any connecting words or ideas.
- When you get to the end, look back and review the flow of your chapters. What else comes to mind?
- Walk around looking at them, getting a bird's eye view. What other words or ideas come to you?

Remember

Fully engage your senses and, as you step from sheet to sheet, think about what the chapter is about and try to get a feel for it.

If you find it difficult to feel, then use another way (seeing, hearing, thinking) to make sense of each chapter

CAUTION: If you are writing an emotionally sensitive book, do not stand on the chapter sheets; observe them by walking alongside. You want to be dissociated from the content.

Brainstorming The Walk

Next, you want to see all of this visually. Before you start, make sure that you have your recording from step it out with you.

Grab Some Tools To Help You With Your Book Outline

- A roll of brown paper
- Post-it notes – lots of colours and shapes
- Coloured pens
- Blue tack if you are putting your paper on the wall
- NoteBook for when inspiration strikes later
- Phone to take photos of your journey and for capturing things that inspire you
- Recording from the previous exercise

Create Your Environment For Creativity

Whenever you do something creative, you need the perfect space where you can just let go and be. Find a room with a spare wall or take over the kitchen or dining room table.

Play music to get you in the mood. Perhaps music that you can sing and dance to. Don't forget the water and staying hydrated – it helps the brain cells and your energy.

Let's Go On A Journey With Our Book Outline

Switch off monkey brain, dance, take a swig of water, and be prepared to discover things you didn't think were in you.

Create Your Road

Draw a road, make it interesting and colourful. Does it undulate, or is it a straight road? Put a picture of you or one representing your book at the top. Divide your road into three. Write beginning, middle and end. This will help you to balance the book and to know how to pace your content.

Listen To Your Recording As You Work

Once you have your road drawn and are ready to go, turn on your recording and start brainstorming.

Core Message

Write the core message of your book at the top of the sheet of paper.

Fun Chapter Titles

Write a silly and fun title for every chapter – just make them up. For example, 'don't eat the petunias' or 'gargoyles and gremlins.'

This gets this out of the way, and you can make sense of your titles later.

Your Stories

Think of stories that you can add that support your content.

What Practical Things Can I Share?

Think questions, observations or thinking points or maybe an exercise or two

Reflections On This Part Of The Journey

That could be gains, losses, gifts, etc.

Key Messages

The key messages are things you want your reader to remember from each chapter or within a particular section. The key message of each chapter must link to the book's core message. You might also call them 'the big idea' or 'the takeaway'. Ask yourself, "what can I share with my reader to help answer their questions?" Review your chapters. What key messages (theme) are there?

Keep reviewing your outline and consider what the key messages are

Use post-it notes to record your thoughts

Questions To Be Answered

As you read and review, ask yourself, "what questions will my reader have?" Add your questions to each chapter.

Call To Action

An effective call to action is part of your overall book and chapter. This is the outcome you want for your reader. Ask yourself, *"what do I want my reader to do as a result of reading this?"* A call to action provides:

- Focus for your book
- Focus for each chapter
- Direction to your readers
- A sense of urgency. Do this now!

Make a note for each chapter of what your call to action is. For example, you could give them an action plan or ask questions to provoke thinking.

Pieces Of Inspiration

Take a break. When you come back, stand and stare at your road. Let everything hang loose, switch off from thinking and gaze as if in a daydream. Next, we want to make this outline much more interesting. But what do you want to change, add or delete before we do? Do that.

Thinking about your journey, what pictures, poems, prose or pieces of inspiration can you add? Go and get them or draw them on. Keep adding to your collage until you feel that it tells your story.

Have You Already Got Content?

If you do, note the content you already have and the gaps. You will be doing a full knowledge audit later.

It's cuppa time again, or maybe a walk. You need some time out to let your brain process this.

Grab Your Phone

Stand and look at your creation, take a deep breath, and then when you are ready, switch on your video and tell your story. Say whatever comes into your mind and trust that your divine inner wisdom knows what the outline and book contents are.

When you have finished, reflect - you need to leave this overnight. So please sleep on your journey.

Next day or when you can, it's time to unravel and create some structure. Take photos, print and put them somewhere you can see them as you listen to your book. Watching the storyline as a video is also very powerful. You will notice things that weren't obvious the first time around.

Mind Mapping

I love mind mapping both freehand and on my computer. With another sheet of brown paper, I sit and listen to my recording and mind map what I hear. Next, I transfer that to a computer-based mind-mapping tool so that I can move things around. As ever, I take lots of reflection time.

Final Review

As you review each chapter, make notes on anything that comes to mind. Then, amend and accept that it may not be perfect – just yet.

Putting It All Together

Once you have your notes from your Step it out exercise, chapter titles, questions, key messages, and call to action, open a document and write it up. Make a copy of what you originally did in the brainstorming from the previous chapter and fill in the gaps. This forms the basis of your synopsis. You will need this for your book proposal.

Different Ways To Get The Outline

You may not want to create your outline in the way that I do, in which case, try one of these: -

- **Index cards:** index cards work well, and I love them because I can lie in bed scribbling and shuffle them around whilst reviewing what I have written. It is easy to slot things in and move them all around
- **Post-it notes:** These are great – find a blank wall and just brainstorm, make sense and use that to refer to when writing up your synopsis

- **Mind mapping software** – iMindmap is what I use. It is fantastic for taking your ideas and being able to flexibly shape your outline
- **Create a PowerPoint or Keynote presentation** of your outline and record yourself delivering it. You can use this as the basis of an online course as well

The key is that you find a way that works for you. I love my approach as I can see the book coming alive. I take time to reflect and approach it in different ways, which helps me make sense of it. This works because you are looking at things in different ways and using different parts of your brain.

Chapter Frameworks / Formats

There are many ways that you can deliver your content. The benefit of frameworks and formats are:

- Structure
- Flow
- Makes it easier to write around
- They help keep you on track
- Saves you time planning and writing your book
- Helps you sell more copies of your book by making the contents of your book obvious to prospective readers – people see things in patterns
- Makes it easier for you to promote your book and convert it into blogs

When you looked at other author's books, you may have noticed that they were writing to a framework. Which did you like? Are you taking a step-by-step approach? Is it a list approach, interviews, Q&As, or a life story? There are many excellent ways to present your content. Use them on their own or in combination with each other.

What, Why, How, What If

Every chapter is split into four sections

- What is this about?
- Why is it important?
- How can I do the same? How also includes questions, case studies and exercises
- What if? Exploring by asking questions or adding in thinking points

It is usually followed by a call to action or an action plan.

Step By Step

The step-by-step or process outline method is commonly used in how-to and self-help books. E.g.

Six weeks to a new you

10 steps to reach your full potential

Five unknown secrets to weight loss success

Five steps from understanding yourself to getting your book self-published

Each chapter, then, is one of the steps, and within each chapter, there will be a logical flow.

Lists

The list approach usually looks something like this, e.g.

101 ways to cook a chicken

99 hot marketing tips for therapists

You could list out your tips or ways in a sequence that appears logical to you, or you might group similar tips together.

Question And Answers/Interviews

If your book was based on a series of questions and answers or interviews, consider presenting these as case studies. You may have theories, action plans, videos, and exercises combined with your case studies.

Life Stories

When the book is based on a part of your life or personal leadership story, the key is to consider what each of your chapters is trying to convey. For example, it may be a sequential set of events, or each chapter might be about a different place or time. The options are endless.

Self-help Memoir

In this example, you can write your story so that you embed the self-help in each chapter, the front part is the story, and the last part is self-help, or you can write a chapter of the story and a chapter of self-help.

Spell It Out

With 'spell it out', you take a word, and each chapter spells it out, e.g. FLOURISH

F- freedom

L - love

O - opportunity

U- understanding

R- reality

I - inspiration

S - senses

H -healing

Storyboarding

My next stage is to prepare for the chapter framework stage and use an artist's A3 pad. I have my recording, photos and my mind map to hand.

You now have a lot of content and ideas for each of the chapters. What you need is a framework so that you can start to make sense of it and make writing easier. This looks like a storyboard you might imagine a scriptwriter would use for a film. The essence of each of your chapters is contained in a box, and you can see clearly how they flow into each other. The storyboard will also help any outsourced team to have a visual of your book.

When You Have Your Framework

When you have chosen one: -

- Work with it
- Test it with two chapters
- Revise
- Perfect

Remember: -

- The core message of the book
- Chapter titles (reflect and review)
- Main chapter idea
- Connect the chapters, step it out – does it flow?
- Determine what questions need answering
- Key messages – link these to the core message
- Call to action

Chapter Titles

We've already looked at titles for your book; now, we want to consider chapter titles. There are two schools of thought about chapter titles; the first is that they can be whatever you want and as whacky as you like. The second is that they convey what the chapter is about using relevant keywords. Remember that people review a table of contents sometimes in their buying decisions, so it may be worth your while spending some time on them so that they emotionally connect to your reader.

Developing chapter titles starts your creative juices flowing and engages your brain to make connections between chapters and consider how they flow into each other. They can be serious or funny and contain action words like changing, controlling, improving, motivating, or achieving. On your initial attempt, the key is to just write the first thing that comes into your head (as in the 'Step it out' exercise); once you have done some more planning and writing, come back and re-craft them.

Imagine you are writing a book on the dieting industry. Your working title might be - Six weeks to a new you. What the dieting industry does not tell you. (Sub-title)

Chapter one of your book on dieting could be a review of the dieting industry and might be called: The dieting industry, a review

Or you may do something more dramatic:

My affair with the diet, learn how my mistakes could save your life

The second title has much more impact and promises what's to come.

With your title and subtitle in mind, create your chapter titles so that they marry with the concept you are trying to convey. The key is to get something written and remember – perfection kills creativity. Always keep your core message in mind. You are now ready to pull together your content.

Write Up All Of Your What's

When you have your titles, outline, and framework, write up all of the chapters whats. Then, simply write this chapter is about and what your reader will learn. Sounds easy, but it will tax your brain and give you lots of clarity.

Add In Your 3 Questions

Do you remember your 30 questions? You can add these to your outline. Write in this chapter, I will be answering these 3 questions.

Actions and Checklist

Create an outline in a way that works for you

Choose a framework, ask why *that* one and how it will convey your message better than the others?

What questions are you answering for your reader?

What are your chapter titles, key messages and call to action?

Do your key messages map to your core message?

Create your book storyboard

Write all of your whats and questions

The Knowledge Audit

In this chapter, you will be introduced to a brilliant concept – the knowledge audit, which will remind you of the content you may already have, the content in your head and what needs researching.

When I wrote Healing Osteoporosis Naturally, I had my story, naturopathic nutrition training and experiences, and books that I had read and then I had to analyse and make sense of a lot of scientific research, which all needed to be cross-referenced and those references added to the book. This is not an easy process, but your readers will want to ensure they can follow up on important information you share. When I wrote Writing To Heal, I had all my course and workshop material, plus experiences and case studies from coaching my clients.

The Knowledge Challenge

Knowing what we know can be a challenge. For your book, you may be thinking of leveraging existing articulated content, existing unarticulated content and formulating new content from your thinking and research. What is already articulated and what is in our heads needs documenting and mapping out.

To make sense of our knowledge, we need to locate it and create a map of where it is and how to access it. To do that, we start with the knowledge formula.

Knowledge = Knowledge (explicit) + Knowledge (tacit)

Explicit = you can touch and feel it because it has already been expressed – you can lick it

Tacit = it's in your head. It is your unconscious competence – the stuff you do without thinking

Knowledge Audit

The knowledge audit is where to find everything that you already have and know. Your job is to find out what you have, where it is and what new things you have to create. Consider what is missing – the gaps. Then evaluate its usefulness for your book. Once you know where everything is and how useful it is, put it in a central location, which might be in a folder, on your computer or online. You need to ask 3 questions: -

- What can you re-purpose?
- What needs to be researched?
- What needs to be written from scratch?

Existing Content (Re-Purpose)

You will be amazed at how much content you already have. Make a list of: -

- Blogs
- Training manuals
- Reports
- Articles
- Transcripts
- Videos and other recordings
- Masterclasses
- Research

The key is to gather and evaluate the usefulness of this in the context of what your book is about. By re-purposing your content, you can make use of the same ideas, thoughts, processes, etc. but create something original and unique from it. Not only can you re-purpose your existing content for your book, but you can also refresh it and develop other products that compliment your book. Finally, consider how else you might use this content when undertaking your knowledge audit. It could be useful for other things.

New Content (Research)

New content is created as a result of identifying gaps in what you know and have. Once you have created your book outline plan and conducted a knowledge audit, it will become obvious where the gaps are. Next, you have to decide what kind of research to undertake. There are two ways to do research:

Secondary Research involves *analysing* information that has already been gathered for another purpose

Primary Research involves *collecting* new information to meet your specific needs

Research for a book can be quite labour-intensive and time-consuming. You will want to cross-check your sources and the validity of your content. Ask yourself how well this research was conducted. Be very critical of your sources. A study of five people is not the same as a study of 5000.

Remember to keep a log of your references and add them to the resources/bibliography at the end of your book. Also, if you have accessed something on the Internet, add the date you accessed it as the content changes.

Interviews

Interviews with experts in your field or with people who are case studies add weight to your book. However, do not produce a book full of interviews with no other content – boring! Instead, choose the people you want to interview based on the value they can add to your book.

Why Conduct Interviews?

- For facts
- Contrast / perspective
- Opinions
- You think your readers would get value from it
- Your book is research-based

How To Conduct A Good Interview

Make sure you research your subject, read their books, websites, blogs, LinkedIn profile and Google them to find out as much as possible. Create questions designed to uncover interesting facts or opinions based on your research. For example, if I were interviewing another author, I would want to know how they write a book, what processes they go through, how they stay on track, etc.

If you are conducting interviews with several specialists, how about constructing a set of five very specific questions? If you are conducting the interview by telephone, email the questions, and if by email only, keep it short. If possible, record your interview in some way.

Set Expectations

When someone agrees to an interview:

- Send them a confirmation e-mail immediately
- Include your questions
- Confirm the interview date and time
- Provide deadlines
- Say thank you and ask how you can help them in return

Books And Magazines

Books and magazines naturally lend themselves to research and being quoted in your work. I can remember when I was doing my MBA. In the two years leading up to my dissertation, I amassed a large pile of books and publications, with little post-it notes marking important points.

Written From Scratch (New Content)

Turning tacit knowledge into explicit. This is where we get what is on our heads out onto paper.

Make a list of your tacit knowledge and make a plan for making it explicit. A great way to do this is to interview yourself with a smartphone or ask someone else to be the interviewer.

Organise Your Content

After you have collated your content, ensure that you organise it all so you have a sense of where each bit will go in your book. Keep your primary idea in mind and the points you are trying to make.

Actions and Checklist

Keeping your outline/storyboard in front of you, conduct your knowledge audit

Where is all of your knowledge? Start pulling it into one place

Decide how you will articulate what's in your head

What new knowledge are you creating? Make a list

What existing content do you have? Make a list of it and markup which chapter it will go in

What additional research do you need to undertake? Create a research action plan

Assess how it is of value to your book

Keep a list of all research papers and books you have referenced, as you will need to add this to the end of your book

Whom will you interview? Create your interview list and start contacting them

Interior Design

In this chapter, we take a brief look at document templates. A template provides the basis for your interior design. It also lets you see your book come alive as you write it.

Many visual writers like to have their document templates (WORD or Docs working space) set up so they can easily navigate their work *and* see it come alive, almost as if it were the end product. Others open WORD and write, coming back to format later. I am in the visual camp, and with WORD, when you turn on the navigation pane, you can see your book outline come alive as you work.

Setting it up first makes life a whole lot easier. If you don't set up a document template with a style sheet, you will end up paying for someone to set it up later and format your book – the interior design. I use WORD for its power and simplicity. What you learn here will be similar to other packages.

What is Interior Design?

Interior book design is the art of creating visually appealing layouts of text and images for the inside of a book. You have to do this before uploading to any book reseller. While you may not undertake the final design creating a document template with a style sheet makes everyone's life easier.

Interior Layout Template

The interior layout template informs us of trim size and margins. Luckily there are websites that have done all the hard work. You can find resources for both print and digital books by Googling.

For a printed book, use Microsoft WORD, either on Windows or Mac. If you search you will find free templates available. Go and download a basic template for your book.

Non-fiction books are typically 6x9 inches. For a digital book, formatting is much simpler. Most publishing sites provide a free guide that you can read online.

If you want your printed book to be styled with different heading formats, highlighted sections, headers and footers, quotes, bold and certain fonts, unless you are technically capable, consider outsourcing to an interior designer.

What Is A Document Template?

A document template is a blueprint for your book. It is set up with the correct page size (trim size), margins, styling options and design for your book. Templates make life easier for the writer and ensure that your book is laid out correctly when you come to print. I like to have all of my templates and style sheets set up before I start to write; I am visual and love to see my work coming alive in the right format as I work. I also find that it helps me to know where I am by making use of the document map (In WORD, view and navigation pane) to navigate my work.

Style Sheets

A style sheet is a standard feature in all word processing programmes that allow you to define the layout and style of the headings and content. Style sheets ensure uniformity and consistency throughout a single document or several documents based on that style. WORD comes with a few pre-defined style sets, which you can modify to suit your needs.

What Styles Might You Need?

- Chapter titles
- Headings 1-5
- The first paragraph, if you are differentiating the first paragraphs from the rest
- Normal paragraph (the first line indented if you like this)
- Quotes
- Bulleted and numbered lists
- Exercises or action plans

Where Would You Find These Styles?

Open a Word document, and they are right in front of you, at the top of your screen. Each of these styles has a set of properties you would set for your book. Then, as you type, you can automatically format as you go along.

Benefits Of Style Sheets

It really is worth learning your word-processing package and utilising all its labour-saving tools.

- Uniformity and consistency
- Easy to make global changes
- Makes creating and updating a table of contents easier
- Makes editing and navigation easier when using the navigation pane/document map

- As a writer, setting up style sheets will save you endless hours of editing

Layout Guide

Once I have downloaded the template, I lay the book out per the usual non-fiction standards. The easiest way is to look at other books and determine what you like. Use this as a guide: -

- Title
- ISBN number
- Dedication
- Legal notices
- Table of contents (hyperlinks if an eBook)
- Content – your chapters
- Resources
- End matter, including an "About the Author" and "More from This Author."

Fonts

There is much debate about the best font, and a book designer who is into typography will be able to tell you why you should use a particular type of font. There are some great articles on fonts, again search and you will find them. Resist all temptation to use too many fancy fonts. All your fonts must be visually balanced. All my books use Roboto and Century Gothic for titles.

Paragraphs

Usually, the first paragraph after a heading is left-aligned, and subsequent ones are the first line indented using the first line hanging option and not by using spaces or the tab key. To make life easy, you can create a new style called the FIRST PARAGRAPH and use NORMAL for the indented paragraphs. Many people these days do not follow the indentation rule: your book, your rules.

Alignment

Justified text for me. Both left and right margins are straight unless it looks weird, and then I manually change that paragraph.

Line Spacing

One and a half or double for eBooks. I have mine set at exactly 18pt for print books. When it comes to headings, play around with what works for you.

Margins

Mirror margins. Go to the resource on the site you want to publish to learn how to set up your margins and gutter for your book.

Take out a book you own. You will see that your thumb fits the outside margin and check how much space there is in the gutter – where the spine is. You will want to ensure that your book will open properly and not obscure the text.

Images

If you need photos, take them yourself or hire a photographer; a professional will add value to the look of your book. Use a designer or illustrator if you need diagrams. Your images must be high resolution and of good quality.

You can use a photo site and buy them. E.g. iStockphoto / Fotolia / Bigstockphoto / DepositPhoto. Look out for photo deals on AppSumo http://www.appsumo.com.

Rules

Make sure you keep a master set of the original images

Do not resize images in WORD. Resize the images outside of your word processor. I use a free online tool www.canva.com

Make sure all images are at least 300dpi for your print book

Resize them to the size you need, and keep a set of the resized images and the originals

You will want to resize your images for an eBook to the smallest size – 96dpi, which you can do within WORD

Headers, Footers And Page Numbers

I create footers with page numbers straight away and leave the other things, like my table of contents, until the end. Then, once the manuscript is at the final draft stage, I will refine my footers and create a table of contents. I tend to not use headers as I find them distracting. But you would add them in the same way that you would footers. In WORD, look for insert; you will see headers and footers in the ribbon.

Page numbers start at the introduction; I prefer them to be centred and in the footer. If you want headers, when you are looking at a 2-page view in WORD, are (as you are looking at the screen), on the left-hand side, my name, centred, and on the right-hand side, the name of the book, centred. And remember to remove your page numbers for eBooks and redo your table of contents, so they are only links.

Page Breaks

Create page breaks by inserting a manual page break (CTRL and ENTER) and not lots of carriage returns. Only put in manual page breaks where you need them, for example, when you want to start a new chapter or a new page or where something specific needs to start on a new page. You do not need a manual page break at the end of each page. Please read the formatting rules for your online publishers website.

Using Icons To Highlight Points And Questions

If you want to draw attention to areas such as questions, exercises or action plans, decide how each of these will be formatted and if there is an icon or picture you will use to draw the eye to them. It is worth considering using a designer to create unique images just for you to fit with your book's overall image. Again, for a eBook, minimal use of these is recommended. Personally, I wouldn't use them in an eBook.

Differences Between Print And Digital Book Formatting

Laying out and formatting a book for self-publishing print and an e-book is different, and you should always read the rules on the sites you want to publish on and use the right tools for the job. If you are using a printer, keep it simple and ask them what they need from you.

You keep your formatting simple for an e-book because you do not know what kind of device your reader will be using. Therefore, your editing plan should contain a process for you to read your book on different devices to get a feel for how it looks and its readability.

DIY Or Professional?

Should you undertake your book's interior layout and format yourself or commission a designer to do it for you? This will depend on you and your ability to use WORD or other software solutions which help you create print books/e-books. If you are technically minded, have an eye for detail and are creative, it should be straightforward for you to develop your interior design and template. If not, then please consider using a skilled professional.

My WRITE! course, which you can find on my website

(www.daledarley.com), will show you how to do all these things.

Actions and Checklist

Set up your document template and style sheet and play with it

Before You Start Writing

In this chapter, we will look at various things to do before you start writing so that you are ready to get your book written and published.

Nail Down A Writing Schedule

When working toward a big, stretchy goal – such as writing a book – it's wise to get yourself into a routine so you build consistent progress daily. In this case, setting aside time each day or week to write is essential to finishing on time and getting your book launched.

Your Writing Schedule

Ideally, you'd be able to set a writing schedule where you work on set days, for a set number of hours, every week. After a week or two, it will become second nature to sit at your computer and get into book writing mode. If your schedule changes from day to day, carve out time at the beginning of each week and schedule those writing blocks so you can still meet your weekly word count goal.

A solid writing routine will include:

- Knowing when and where you're going to write
- Choosing ONE place where you exclusively write this book
- Eliminating all distractions during this time

Choosing one place to write is simply part of the routine you're developing. You're training your mind that when you sit down, it's time to write and focus on your outline and how you can serve your readers. Eliminating distractions may seem obvious but be diligent about turning off your notifications, closing extra windows, and turning your phone to Do Not Disturb mode. Then, go a step further and put your phone in another room so you're not tempted to take a look at it.

Start by creating a weekly writing schedule. Look at your calendar and start blocking off time for your non-negotiable items. If you use an online digital calendar, you can create different colours for different activities.

Then look and see what time blocks are left open for writing. If it's the same time every day, wonderful! That makes it extra easy to remember. If you need to get up early or stay up late to write, that's perfectly fine. So long as you're putting in the effort instead of making excuses for not writing.

When necessary, be creative about your schedule. For example, if you go to the gym every Monday, Wednesday and Friday morning, maybe you choose to write on Tuesday and Thursday morning at the same time you'd normally go to the gym on the other days. Even if all you can carve out is 20 minutes per week, you can still get it into your calendar—and adjust your word count accordingly. You can use this time to write or edit.

Remember to track your progress and celebrate your small wins. Reaching your word count goal is worth celebrating, so create a spreadsheet to track your progress for each completed writing session. Include the date and the number of words you managed to write. This will not only keep you accountable, but you'll also be able to 'see' the fruits of your labour.

Draft Your Book When You Can

And Where You Are

While ideally, you'll be able to hit your desk to write a certain amount of hours per day or week, the truth is, this isn't always possible. Sometimes life gets in the way, and the best intentions are crushed.

But have no fear... you can work around emergencies, illness, or other life entanglements. The good news is that another way has been proven to work for many authors: writing their book on their phone or tablet.

Yes, you read that right. There's literally no right or wrong way to write your book. It's all about finding what works for you! Even if you think, "There's no way I'll write on my phone," I urge you to take these steps to ensure your outline and draft are saved in the cloud and that you know how to access them on different devices. It's better to be prepared with a backup and never need it rather than need it and be without.

Try a cloud-based writing tool like Google Docs that you can use on multiple devices. Or save your WORD files in your Google Drive, OneDrive or Dropbox. You can create a Book Folder and keep your outline and draft together.

NOTE: Some authors choose to write their actual book right in their outline. Others prefer to create a FRESH document for writing their actual book. Choose what works best for you! I like to create a fresh chapter at the start and, after editing, compile it into one document. I use the navigation feature in WORD to see the flow.

Now that you have access to your documents across multiple devices, you have the freedom to write during stolen moments, including at your child's music practice or watching your partner play football.

Brainstorm 'Stolen Moments' You Have In Your Usual Week

When do you have a small pocket of free time that you could dedicate to your book? Thinking about these moments in advance can help you remember when the time comes.

Ways To Get To The First Draft

There are several ways that you can get your book written. These include: -

- Write it yourself
- Drip your content on your blog
- Talk it and transcribe
- Work a ghostwriter
- Work with a coach who will interview you

Write It Yourself

As I love writing, this would be my first choice, followed by talking it or a combination of the two methods. You will need to put aside daily time and write for an hour before doing anything else for the day or write for several hours over a series of weekends. Having your outline in front of you as you write is helpful.

Drip It Out As Custom Content, Week-By-Week

Book publishing has changed dramatically over the years. Once upon a time, the only way to get published was if a traditional book publisher liked your manuscript. Then along came online publishers and the advent of self-publishing. With the internet's reach, you can drip-feed your content to your readers before your book is even finished.

Releasing your book chapter by chapter is another hack to get your book done quickly because it takes the pressure off from having to write a whole book at once. Focusing on each chapter allows you to set shorter, seemingly more manageable goals. Plus, you'll be able to start collecting feedback on your writing right away.

I recommend blogging your book to build your brand and attract the right people to your website. Dripping your book content is simply a way to market it before launching it. Remember that no one is going to sit and read your entire blog. They much prefer to have a book.

One of the things I do is blog my books. I create a plan for each chapter and then put out a series of blogs. It will be no surprise that I have a course called Blog Your Book.

Your advance readers can also help create buzz around your

book launch and are prime candidates for giving a testimonial or review. Remember to create a giveaway so that you can collect email addresses so that when the time is right, you can create your book launch team.

There are quite a few ways you could drip out your content to readers, including:

1. Blog your book and write each chapter as a series of blog posts. You use WordPress, Medium or even LinkedIn to share your book content

2. Turn your book chapters into a paid, monthly subscription, course or program. You might deliver the month's chapter in a colourful PDF, with some videos, for example, for $10/month until you're done. This not only gives you an incentive to finish, but it provides your audience with a "first look" at your book long before it gets published. They can also provide you with feedback to help you "hone" your book before you self-publish it another way

3. Share as YouTube videos with a sign-up for a free giveaway, and then encourage those people to become a part of your launch team

Even if you don't want to drip the entire book, publish the first chapter online to give people a feel for your writing style and introduce yourself as a qualified author. You could also record the first chapter for those who prefer to listen to books. Recording a chapter to compliment a giveaway is a great idea in the lead-up to a launch.

Will Dripping Content Work For Me?

How do you feel about dripping your content – chapter by chapter – for free online?

- I like that idea. It will be a grand experiment.
- I've already given away too much content for free; why should I give my book away, too?

Who do I want to read it?

- Everyone!
- My email list only (exclusive offer)
- Anyone willing to pay a subscription

Will this tactic motivate you to stick with your writing commitment? Why or why not?

Personally, I love using my blog to help me to write my book.

Blog Your Book Challenge

Take a 30-day challenge and write 30 blogs in at least 1000 to 1500 words in one month. If you like a challenge, this will definitely keep you on track. This is also a great way to pre-market your book.

Talk And Transcribe

If you're a natural-born chatterbox who hates to write, another hack for writing a book is to skip the writing altogether and voice record your book instead. There are multiple ways you could do this, including:

- On your phone (voice-to-text in your Notes app, then copy it into your outline)
- In Google Docs, use "Voice Typing"
- Programs like Dragon Naturally Speaking and talk your book
- Recording yourself on Zoom, Screencast or Loom, then having the audio transcribed (Rev.com is one paid option, Otter.ai has a free version – I have the paid version. You can also use Otter on your phone)

You can even have someone else interview you if talking to yourself on Zoom feels weird.

Once you receive your transcript, you'll edit from that first while choosing which parts to include in the book. Even though you're an expert, always edit your transcript. For example, you might think of a different way to explain things, or maybe you included a rant that doesn't have a place in your book. Make your edits, copy and paste them into the working manuscript, and then continue recording (or writing) the next chapter.

The beauty is that you can switch between transcription and writing fairly easily. Transcribing is another option if you don't like typing on your phone but want to make the most of your time away from your computer. Additional editing might be necessary as our speaking tone often doesn't match our writing tone. However, you'll save time with transcription in the long run. As a side note, I hate editing transcriptions – so check if this works for you or not.

Experiment with recording your voice with each of the dictation options listed above. For example, try speaking one piece of your outline or reciting the whole thing. Does one option feel good and natural for you? Do you like how the transcription came out? Weigh the pros and cons of each, then decide if you'll use one either during your regular writing schedule or those 'stolen moments' moving forward. Ask these questions after you experiment with each of the options:

- What worked?
- What didn't work?
- Was it easy to use?
- Where did the audio get filed?
- What are the next steps after recording?

Use A Ghostwriter To Finish Your Book

Consider hiring a ghostwriter if you've read all the above and still don't know if you have time to write your book. Even with the biggest cheering squad in town, this book process will be a drain if you don't enjoy writing. Ghostwriters can save the day, but hiring can also be expensive.

Ghostwriters will help you outline and then write the entirety of your book based on your ideas in a voice that sounds like yours.

Then, after the book is written and paid for, you'll receive the rights to the book so you can publish it under your own name.

Why Wouldn't A Ghostwriter Want Credit For The Book?

Because they entered into the contract without any expectation of receiving credit. So long as you pay the ghostwriter and they understand the terms of your contract, the finished product is yours to do with as you like. It's no different than hiring a copywriter to write your sales page or an advertising agency creating television commercials for their clients.

I often do a lot of developmental editing and writing for clients and never take the credit because when I am writing for others, their voice comes through me. My goal is to help them have a book they are truly proud of, which makes me feel good.

If you decide to go this route, interview multiple writers. If this book represents you and your company, each candidate should appreciate the importance of a job well done. Ask about their experience, their turnaround time, and their availability. Even if they promise your book in two weeks (unlikely), they might not be available for another 9 months. I would expect them to be able to write 30-40,000 in three months.

Work With A Coach

A coach will work with you all the way through your book. This stage is extremely valuable. Your coach will use the synopsis to guide them and ask questions about your chapter ensuring that there is flow from one to another.

Actions and Checklist

Nail down your writing schedule

Consider how you will get the first draft written

Write Your First Draft

In this chapter, you will test your chapter outline, framework, and plan by writing some of one chapter and then shaping it into a format and writing formula for the rest of the book.

"Most people who bother with the matter at all would admit that the English language is in a bad way, but it is generally assumed that we cannot by conscious action do anything about it. Our civilisation is decadent, and our language – so the argument runs – must inevitably share in the general collapse. It follows that any struggle against the abuse of language is a sentimental archaism, like preferring candles to electric light or hansom cabs to aeroplanes. Underneath this lies the half-conscious belief that language is a natural growth and not an instrument which we shape for our own purposes." (Orwell 1946). George very kindly goes on to tell us that there are six rules to adhere to: -

- Never use a metaphor, simile, or another figure of speech that you are used to seeing in print.
- Never use a long word where a short one will do.
- If it is possible to cut a word out, always cut it out.
- Never use the passive where you can use the active.
- Never use a foreign phrase, a scientific word, or a jargon word if you can think of an everyday English equivalent.
- Break any of these rules sooner than say anything outright barbarous.

First Chapter Trial Write

Before you panic and think that I want you to write the whole of any chapter, I do not. Instead, I want you to **take one of your chapters, which are well outlined, and write for one to two hours.** In that time, try to write a bit in all sections. In this way, you can get a sense of how your chapter layout will flow, whether your framework is suitable and where you need to make adjustments.

When you have written what you can, take 20 minutes off. Then, refine the chapter layout, so you have a writing template for the rest of your book. You are looking to create a formula which will make it easy for you to write all of your chapters.

Is it clear, and does your writing flow in this pattern? If not, re-jig it until it works for you. For example, you might start with a story or a case study, then move into 'what' and 'why', followed by some exercises which illustrate your strategies, and then conclude with another case study and some thinking points.

You may start by painting a big picture, move into more detail and then go back to the big picture. You might start with something positive, use the middle to cover off difficult subjects and then move back to a positive position. Alternatively, start with a difficult piece and end on a positive piece (my preference)

Does your writing create bridges and links between theory, stories and exercises? Does it ask questions to get your reader thinking and exploring?

Other Points To Consider

Keep each chapter in a separate file (WORD or PAGES document); it is easier to work on smaller chunks of work.

Let go of any attachment you have to what you have written;

when you come back, you will be able to edit with clarity and focus

Don't let grammar, spelling, or punctuation get in the way of your writing. Just write. Remember, the magic comes in the editing

Add, change or review chapter titles and subheadings as they come to you. These can be changed later. I often use my questions as subheadings

If you are unclear if your chapter style and layout work, ask someone. What I do for my clients is read through it considering learning styles, looking for flow, structure, story start and end, and making sure exercises work and whatever else might enhance the copy

I have an outline using the what, why, how, what if framework in front of me as I write each chapter. This helps me by making sure I have answered all of these questions.

When you have worked on one chapter, try it with another. How does it flow? What changes do you need to make to the framework?

In WORD, use the READ ALOUD option under REVIEW. It's kind of strange but very helpful

Read your chapter aloud, as this will give you a feel for what you are trying to say. Better still, video yourself and listen back

The First Draft, Here You Come

Congratulations on getting this far. That is quite an achievement. Next, you will look at how to get your first draft completed.

Forget Introductions – Just Write

Forget introductions, one of the reasons we get stuck writing is that we are trying to work out our introduction. So, after you have planned your outline, get on with writing the content. In other words – just write.

Chapter Outline Plan Reminder: -

- What is this chapter about?
- What are the questions your reader wants you to answer?
- What are your key messages? What can you tell your reader that will help to answer their questions?'
- What is the outcome of this chapter?
- Do your key messages map to your core message?
- What are your subheadings?
- What is your call to action? What do you want your reader to do as a result of reading this chapter?

Getting To The First Draft: Rules

- If you haven't nailed down your writing schedule, go and do it…

- Make time every day to write, set goals and celebrate often
- Record each chapter and listen before you write
- Keep your chapter story in front of you as you write
- Keep a picture of your ideal reader where you can see it
- Find the right environment to write
- Commit to getting your first draft done by a set date
- Get someone to hold you accountable
- Get your resources and support systems in place before you start
- Adapt your thinking and adopt a writer's mindset
- Turn off the critical voices. What do they know about first drafts anyway?
- Shoot your inner perfectionist in the head; constant worrying about your first draft will get you nowhere
- Your first draft is just that, a foundation, giving you a chance in later drafts to turn it into something great
- Think big picture; forget getting bogged down in too much detail. For all you detail people, come back to the question you are answering; ask yourself, "do I have 'scope creep'?" For you, big picture people, remember at some point, you will have to add detail
- Don't worry about grammar, spelling or punctuation at this stage. Just get your ideas out
- Formatting doesn't matter unless you need a visual structure to 'see' where you are going, in which case, use

a simple layout. Interior design comes later (except if you are me…)
- Flow doesn't always come, so write when you can or move onto an area that does flow. Writing doesn't have to be linear
- If you are stuck, change your focus and write a blog that could be used in your book
- Keep a journal to record your ideas and reflections
- Writing is hard work. When the going gets tough, remember your commitment and just get on with it

First Drafts Suck

When you get to the end of your first draft, elation is usually followed by embarrassment as you read what you have written. Get over it and congratulate yourself on coming this far.

Often, when I read the first draft, I expect to be embarrassed, but I am amazed at what has come out. Plus, I am thankful that I have something to work from. It's always better than a blank page.

Quality Over Quantity

When I wrote the dissertation for my coaching qualification, I wrote 30,000 words when only 6,000 to 10,000 were required. I was absorbed by the subject and unloaded my thoughts. That was my first draft, and I suffered from a bad dose of 'scope creep'. This happens to me every time.

- First drafts will always be a stream of unconsciousness, and that's ok
- To get to quality, you have to be brutal when you edit
- Never throw away the work you discard. It will always come in handy later

Actions and Checklist

Write your first chapter, leave it, and reflect. Give yourself a pat on the back (or some chocolate); you have the first draft of one of your chapters and know how to get there

Decide how you are going to get your first draft written and put it in your plan so that you achieve it

If you are writing it yourself, either write for 1-2 hours a day before you do anything else or use 2-5 weekends

If you are using an outsourced service, create a specification of your expectations and get several quotes

Turn Your Book Into A Business

In this chapter, I invite you to ponder – what else can you use your book for and how to use it to create a business?

Before creating my book, I like to consider what potential products and services I can create. But, like all businesses, I have done things back to front, like leaping in with a book and not really thinking about what else I can make from it and how to build a business around it.

When I wrote this book, you know I wanted to use it to build my brand and give it away at workshops. Unfortunately, things were different when I first wrote it, and I missed many opportunities.

Start to consider how you could write a book to launch a business. Ask yourself what kind of business this could be? I have an online school – The Soul Writers Academy, which has lots of eBooks, courses and different group coaching programs. I couldn't run a membership, but for other people, this is perfect. You may love to speak, and the book will support this for you.

Start by brainstorming what your business could look like and think about what gives you energy and what drains your energy.

When creating products and services, I think about my end-to-end vision and mission. And most importantly, how does my book fit with my business goals?

You, like me, will want to produce excellent products and services from your book ideas, where you'll establish authority in your niche and be seen as the go-to expert. As well as this, you want to be able to satisfy different client's needs and price points.

Let's move forward and brainstorm all the potential products and services you have and would like to have, even if they are not on your radar.

Product Development

This all sounds a bit technical, right? However, in my product management days, I had to look at many things before taking a product to market.

- Finding the right opportunity (market research)
- Planning (creating your book plan and outline)
- Designing your products and services, including add-ons and service commitments
- Go to market strategies
- Feedback

The bottom line is you want a well thought out range of products and services that are easy to buy and consume. A good first impression means you deliver against what you promise most effectively. Your clients can buy what they want and need, delivering great value and the promised outcomes. When you do this, you will most likely keep them onboard with you.

Products And Services

Product management is the day-to-day management of your products/services at all product lifecycle stages. These are typically the four stages:

- Embryonic

- Growth
- Maturity
- Decline

When creating their products, most businesses rarely think of this in the excitement of launching something new. I know how dated courses can look a few years after being first written. Some of my courses went from maturity to dead in the water, and others I revitalised. For example, one of my older courses had lectures over 20 minutes. These are now 5 to 10 minutes long so that they are easier to consume, and I added in new material, which was more in line with newer thinking and concepts.

Sometimes, I have gone straight from embryonic to decline and kicked myself in the process. But as I always say, it's a learning process, even if time-consuming. So I hope to save you this pain.

When you look at the range of products and services you have and hope to deliver, which stage is each at? The key here is to consider the brand new sparkly thing and how you can use older products that may need tweaking in your roadmap.

Product Levels

Again in the heady world of marketing, products are usually described as having three levels:

- the **CORE** product (benefits)
- the **ACTUAL** product (this speaks for itself)

- and the **AUGMENTED** product (added value)

The CORE product is NOT the tangible, physical product. You can't touch it. That's because the core product is the BENEFIT of the product that makes it valuable to your clients.

The ACTUAL product is the tangible, physical product. You can get some use out of it.

The AUGMENTED product is the non-physical part of the product. It usually consists of lots of added value, for which you may or may not pay a premium.

Features And Benefits

With your list of products and services, all beautifully categorised by lifecycle, start to consider the features and benefits of each product or service you intend to create from your blueprint. I know you don't have it yet, but this will help give you more clarity. Additionally, it should be easier because you are using your story to underpin this.

Features include a workbook, an assessment, a well-structured outline, a FaceBook group, weekly calls, email support and 24-hour access.

Benefits include bouncing out of bed on a Monday morning because they have a job they love. Landing a job you love. Attracting the right clients. Stress reduction and finding inner peace. The way to look at benefits is to say which means that.

Where Are They On The Product Lifecycle?

In reality, very few products follow the prescriptive cycle mentioned earlier. The length of each stage varies enormously. The decisions you make can change the stage, for example, from maturity to decline by price-cutting. Not all products go through each stage. Some go from introduction to decline. It is not always easy to tell which stage the product is in. By listing your product and services ideas, looking at what you already have, and considering features and benefits, you can start to ask some great questions:

- What if any products/services need to be phased out?
- What if any products/services can be added to the roadmap?
- What products or services can you see that might be more in demand in future?
- What is the general state of health of each product/service and the product mix as a whole?

You will also need to consider which products will give you the greatest opportunity for profitability. Your MVP (minimum viable product) might be free or very low cost. Its task is to lead and encourage your clients to want to consume other products and services. You'll have to consider what is potentially on your product roadmap in conjunction with price and profitability. Sometimes you just have to let things go because they are not what is creating business for you. Remember that nothing is lost; you can probably reconfigure something once you have thought about why it didn't work and release it in another way.

Benefits Of Having A Range Of Integrated Products And Services

- You are providing a variety of ways and price points for clients to enrol in your services.
- Create a variety of ways for clients to engage with you according to their preferred learning styles and the time available
- Offer a variety of engagement touchpoints, which allows you to expand your reach and geographic impact
- Scale your business beyond a one-on-one hourly revenue approach
- Keep your work fresh so that you are working around similar issues - but in different formats

Potential Products

Here are some ideas for you. You may, like me, have lots of these things which might be reusable or not and worth creating. So when you look at these, why you would add them to your business.

Lead Magnet

This is a high-quality item you give away in return for an email address, also known as a lead magnet. Your lead magnet needs to be designed to filter in leads who might become the right prospective clients. This is why you do the work first to identify who that might be.

This gift needs to be related to your book and add value. You want to give something away which whets your potential reader/client's appetite and leaves them wanting more. The lead magnet's objective is to get your potential clients to opt in so that you can nurture the relationship.

When your potential clients sign up, they can see what is coming. You may want to invite them to enrol on a mini-course, take them through a quiz, or give them a workbook, checklist, template, chapter of a book or a blueprint checklist. All of which are designed to give them a flavour of what is to come. The key is to keep it simple while full of value, and you have a clear call to action.

Don't forget the thank you page where you can invite them to your group or connect elsewhere on social media. Also, think about the follow-up email sequence or potential upsells.

A word on upsells. If you are anything like me, I want to grab the thing I want, and I do not want to go through a barrage of get this now; it's going away, followed by yet another and yet another upsell. This puts me off, and I generally abandon the lead magnet. So think carefully about your brand and your clients.

Place your lead magnet on your website, within your blog posts, other content, and in the first section of your book. You can still place links inside LinkedIn and Medium posts and your social media profiles if you don't have a website.

What Makes A Good Lead Magnet?

- The perceived value. Your lead magnet should be perceived as something highly valuable which leads to an outcome and solves a problem
- Instant gratification: Your potential clients want the answer to a problem immediately. If your lead magnet can fill that gap, you will build an email list in no time
- Demonstrates what makes you different. When your client consumes your lead magnet, it needs to demonstrate why you?

It's important to grow your email list as you do not own any social media network. They could disappear overnight. The lead magnet is an important first step in getting clients.

E-book

E-books make great lead generation tools. Consider what content you can wrap into an e-book and use as a lead magnet or something you charge for but do not charge a lot. If free, it will differ in length and content from your paid e-book, which is probably in the 5000 to 12000 words bracket.

Your e-book could be based on a long blog post, which you created as a big idea based on your book idea. Some people don't want to read long posts and will jump at the chance to get all of your juicy ideas as an e-book. Perhaps the first chapter of a potential book could act as an e-book or content that you had considered for your book but have ripped out. I never delete anything, and I am always thinking about how I can repurpose it with purpose.

For example, in one book, I had a section on how to be a better writer and decided that these 5000 words would lend themselves to an e-book rather than the main book. You can offer your free eBook from various places on your website, on freebie days in social media groups and on all your social media channels.

Mini-course

Mini-courses are wonderful. Typically low priced, and they could form the basis of a free or paid for challenge. What could you create that takes a potential client through your process, gives them an outcome and whets their appetite for more? These are anything from 7 to 14-day steps. This could also be your minimum value product (MVP).

Blog Your Book

When you have your outline, you may decide that you want to blog your book rather than sit down and write it all in one go. I often blog my book as I write it for clarity and to test the content with my potential clients. When I have written my book, I'll often reblog it and use the call to action to drive book and/or course/program sales. This approach also improves your searchability and visibility.

Turn Your Book Into A Course

This is a logical step. Once you have a book, creating a course is so easy – ok easyish… This gives you the chance to engage with potential clients who like to work alone. However, it can also give you leads for your book, coaching and programs.

Create A Brilliant Program

Your signature program falls naturally out of your book outline and synopsis. It is not as time-consuming to write as a book or a course, as you can create workbooks for each section which you deliver as you go along. A signature program is your step-by-step process or system (like your book), which helps your client achieve the desired outcome. It is usually based on your story and is your reason for being product, which shows your client how to, step by step, overcome personal and professional challenges. And, of course, it has your fingerprint all over it. This is your unique way of providing a solution to a problem, including who you are and what you believe in. There are many reasons for creating a signature program, including:

- Standing out from the crowd
- Giving back through sharing your learning

- Increased revenue in a shorter period by delivering to a group with a specific problem rather than 121
- Attract clients who need to solve one specific problem which you have the knowledge, skills and experience to do
- Be more visible, be seen as an expert and demonstrate the authority of your message
- It is a repeatable process
- Declutter your processes, create focus and clarity
- Increases your confidence because you know that you are changing lives

You need to consider sharing the process they will be going through, how you will be doing that, how long they will work with you, and what extra they will get. I always give away my course, so there is a place to get advice during the program and when it is all over. Often I will keep the group open for ongoing peer support too. These are great if you like shorter times with a group of clients.

One-on-One Coaching

As well as the products outlined above, many coaches and consultants like to offer an individual coaching program that naturally follows the book's flow. Interestingly, when you analyse your coaching, the questions you get asked the most are the themes you coach on. Again, these naturally feed into your book idea.

VIP Days

VIP days are intensive deep dives with you, where you deliver what is in your book over 1-5 days or a series of half days. You can give your potential client a menu of your chapters and use these to create a specific day or days.

Retreats And Virtual Retreats

Retreats enable your clients to get away from it all. They are usually in delicious surroundings with great food, services and experiences. With a move to more online work, you can create virtual retreats that give the feeling of getting away and being focused on one thing. I, for example, offer virtual book writing retreats. The benefit of virtual retreats is that my clients can come on a retreat from anywhere.

Membership Programs

This is simply a program where people join for a monthly fee, and you deliver regular content to them. So if you like to create long-lasting communities, this will be for you.

Choosing Your Delivery Method

What comes to mind when you look at the list of ideas above and others you may have added? Yikes, where will I find the energy or yay, or I know exactly what I am going to do? It's worth mentioning here that you need to consider what gives you energy and what sucks your energy. If you love groups, great a group program will delight you. If you don't, you will dread delivering it, and your clients will know. How much time or other available resources do you have? Not only do you need to consider your needs, but also those of your clients.

Your Product Roadmap

Every business knows that you cannot develop products without a roadmap, including what the product is, why you are creating it, how you will create it, what resources you need and when and how you will launch it. The product roadmap must fit with your business model and make sense for you.

Actions and Checklist

Make a list of potential products and services that can flow from your book

Assess each in terms of desire and energy

Design an outline product roadmap

Make a shortlist and reflect

About The Author

Dale works with her clients to help them discover how to use their story to discover their reason for being and how to convert that into profitable products and services.

She ensures that her client's brand, business and book are aligned. And if it is a personal story about how that will serve the client in the best way. She always ensures that her clients get their desired outcome and more.

She believes that writing heals, and indeed many of her clients come to her to write business books, only to discover that there are elements of their life meandering through the themes that need clarity. She works to help them overcome any stumbling blocks and find a way to heal these through their writing.

Many years ago, she decided that her mission was to help people tell their stories and turn them into published books and other products and services. She left a highly successful marketing career and now works with people like you to become published authors and build their personal brand with books, blogs, and online courses.

Dale is also a highly regarded personal branding expert. She will help you find your voice and inspirational message and turn what you know into something bigger than your book.

Outside of writing and coaching, you can find her walking her beautiful dogs, Marley and Angel (all rescues) and eating cake – healthy, of course.

When will you write your book?

Please contact me if you are inspired and want to write a book. You can contact me by email at DD@DaleDarley.com. and www.daledarley.com

Resources

Sign up for the worksheets

You will find your worksheets here:

https://daledarley.com/pynfbw-resources/

Group Coaching And Teaching Programmes

I coach globally via Zoom and face-to-face. You can find everything on www.daledarley.com.

www.ingramcontent.com/pod-product-compliance
Lightning Source LLC
Chambersburg PA
CBHW071711170526
45165CB00005B/1974